MIDDLE EAST OIL
ISSUES AND PROBLEMS

By The Same Author

MIDDLE EAST OIL ISSUES AND PROBLEMS

Benjamin Shwadran

SCHENKMAN PUBLISHING CO.
Cambridge, Mass.

Copyright © 1977
Schenkman Publishing Company, Inc.
3 Mt. Auburn Place
Cambridge, Massachusetts 02138

Library of Congress Cataloging in Publication Data

Shwadran, Benjamin
Middle East Oil
   1. Petroleum industry and trade — Near East.
2. Near East — History — 20th century. I. Title.
HD9576.N36S55   338.2'7'2820956   77.2982
ISBN 0-87073-597-7
ISBN 087073-598-5 pbk.

Printed in the United States of America

Contents

1 Introduction

The energy crisis which in October 1973 threw the world into a panic, and for which no solution has as yet been found, was and is in reality the Middle East oil crisis.[1] Four paramount factors emerge from the development of the oil industry in the region which have decisively contributed to the crisis: oil production, oil reserves, oil revenue and oil prices; all four grew, in a comparatively short period of time, into legendary proportions. In 1955, for instance, the entire region produced 6,340,000 tons of oil, and they made up 3.3% of world production, and in 1973 the region produced 1,045,000,000 tons, and they made up 37.5% of world production. The estimate of Middle East oil reserves in 1945 was 18 billion barrels, in 1973 it reached 400 billion barrels. One authoritative source gave it as 56% of world reserves, while another, equally as authoritative, put it at 62.7% of world reserves. Direct oil revenue of the region amounted in 1955 to $898 million; the estimated revenue for 1974 ran from $90 to 110 billion. The average price of a barrel of crude oil in the Middle East in January 1971 was $1.80; in October 1975 it went up to $12.80; in December 1976 Saudi Arabia and the United Arab Emirates increased prices by 5%, and the other producing countries increased oil prices by 10%.

These few statistics are sufficient to demonstrate the enormous proportions of the Middle East oil problem. However, these economic and financial aspects of the problem are overshadowed by the very seriously troubled international political situation, which is in essence a major outcome of the Middle East oil crisis.

The development of the oil industry in the region since the Arab-Israel June 1967 war hastened, no doubt, the emergence of the crisis in its present proportions. An attempt will be made in the ensuing chapters, to deal with the outstanding issues and developments during the period from 1967 until today, and discuss them in terms of the region as a whole.

(1) The Middle East, for oil statistical purposes includes, in this study, the following countries: Turkey, Syria, Lebanon, Jordan, Israel, Iran, Iraq, Saudi Arabia, the Persian Gulf Principalities and Egypt. In the general discussion of the oil issues and problems Libya and Algeria are also included.

The story of the Middle East oil industry unfolds in the form of two long major struggles. One among the Powers themselves and the other between the producing countries and the concessionary companies. The first was to obtain oil concessions for the respective companies to exploit the oil resources in the different states and territories of the region. It commenced practically at the beginning of our century, when it became evident that there were oil resources in Mesopotamia, then part of the Ottoman Empire, and today Iraq. Involved at first were England, Holland, Germany and the United States. The Europeans succeeded by uniting in preventing the Americans from penetrating an area which they considered as their preserve. Their three ambassadors pressured the Sultan's government in Constantinople, and the concession was granted to the Turkish Petroleum Company, which was dominated by the British Anglo-Persian Oil Company. At the end of World War I the Germans were eliminated and replaced by the French, who were given a secondary role, while the Americans returned to play a major role. The withdrawal of the Russians from the area, after the 1917 revolution, and the collapse of the Ottoman Empire left Britain as the only great military Power in the region. A bitter and prolonged struggle took place between England and the United States for economic exploitation rights in the region. At the end, the Americans came out victorious, and they obtained the lion's share of the oil concessions in the Middle East.

At the end of World War II the Soviet Union returned to the region and demanded oil concessions. However, the strong, stubborn and determined stand taken by the United States prevented the Soviet Union from obtaining any concession in northern Iran which it considered its security zone. The Soviet Union succeeded, however, in blocking the Western Powers from establishing themselves, through oil concessions, in northern Iran along its border.

The last arrangement between the two major and decisive contestants for oil concessions in the area occurred in 1954 when the Americans obtained 40% of the Iranian concession—after Iran nationalized the oil industry in 1951—in the newly organized international Consortium which took over the concession from the Anglo-Iranian Oil Company. From that year until 1973 the pattern of the distribution of concessions remained constant, although not all the Western Powers were satisfied with it.

The strategic importance of the Middle East, because of both its geographic location and the oil it contains, increased especially from the time of World War I and reached a certain peak in World War II. All the three major allies—England, the United States and the Soviet Union— united in their determination to protect and defend the region as the major channel for war supplies to reach Russia, and above all to prevent the enemy from overrunning it and using the oil resources to continue the war against the allies.

In the post-World War II period when the world Powers began to group into East and West blocs, the Middle East and its oil gained primary importance. During the first post-war years the Western Powers attempted to organize different military groupings and organizations for the defence of the region in which the countries therein would actively participate. These attempts, however, failed, but the strategic importance of the region did not diminish and the position of the allies did not change, except that the villain of the drama changed: Germany was replaced by the Soviet Union. Slowly, for a variety of good and solid reasons, the United States' partners withdrew and she remained the only Great Power to challenge the Soviet Union. The inter-Power struggle was no longer for oil concessions, nor between allies, but a battle between the two Super-powers, each striving to gain influence and control of the region, or at least prevent the opponent from establishing itself in the area. In this contest, the role of the nations of the area, especially the oil producers, assumed extraordinary significance.

The second struggle was between the oil producing countries, the grantors of the concessions, and the concessionary companies which exploited the oil resources of the area. This contest began, in fact, immediately after World War I between Persia (Iran) and the Anglo-Persian (Iranian) Oil Company; and after concessions were granted in the other countries and territories, between the various producers and the different companies.

After the producers realized and understood on the one hand the extent of the concessions, and on the other hand the very meagre share which they obtained from the exploitation of their huge natural resources, they tried to change the terms of the concessions, in order to enlarge their royalties, increase the employment of local residents especially in the senior and administrative positions, and to partici-pate in the management of the companies.

For various reasons—historical, international, political and eco-nomic—the process of the gains of the producing countries was slow and the achievements were very limited. However, the more the producers proceeded with their efforts the more determined and per-sistent they became. In the early 'fifties they succeeded in increasing their share—which was until then only 16% of the companies' production profits or 4-6 British shillings per ton, or some com-bination of both—to 50% of production profits. These 50% were divided into two elements, 12.5% as royalty, and the balance as income tax. The basis of calculating the profits was the posted price of oil agreed upon by both sides, although the real determiners were the companies. The posted prices were not always the real prices but established for the purpose of reckoning the tax.

The big jump in the income of the producers from $193.5 million in 1950 to $898 million in 1955, more than a fourfold increase, brought satisfaction to the producers and instituted good relations between them and the companies; in some instances the relations were even friendly. The period of the 'fifties will no doubt be described as the golden age in the history of the relations of the oil industry in the Middle East, especially after the settlement of the Iranian conflict.

However, as the producers became accustomed to their ever growing rate of oil revenue, and they prepared huge government budgets and grandiose long-range economic development programs, the struggle began anew when the companies cut, at the end of the 'fifties and early in 'sixty, the posted prices. They argued that the oil markets were satiated as a result of the pressure of the producers to increase output. The battle between the two became acute indeed.

Out of this renewed battle came into being, in the early 'sixties, under the initiative of Iraq and with the help of Venezuela, the Organization of Petroleum Exporting Countries (OPEC). It tried as the producers' collective instrumentality to restore the cuts in the posted prices and thus increase the revenue.

Because of purely objective factors OPEC was incapable of attaining its aim. The world demand for oil was much lower than the supply, and the organization was not in a position of forcing the companies to restore the cuts in the posted prices. The companies held all the cards: technical know-how, the huge financial resources necessary to operate and expand the industry, the refining plants, the transportation facilities and especially the international markets. Since the major oil companies possessed oil resources in the United States they could regulate production without being exclusively dependent on the Middle East oil. Moreover, in spite of the official competition between the various oil companies, they operated, especially in the price structure, as a strong and well organized monopoly; while the producers, in spite of their membership in OPEC, each acted in its own interests and was not ready to make any sacrifices for the good of the organization as a whole. All the members together and each one separately, were dependent on the companies, and without them the huge quantities of oil could not be marketed.

To be sure, during the 'sixties OPEC obtained a number of limited concessions from the companies for its members. The companies deducted a percentage of the posted price as the producers' contribution for the oil sales promotion. The fourth conference of OPEC, which convened at Geneva in April, 1962, decided to take steps to eliminate this contribution. In the middle of 1963 Iran announced that the Consortium had agreed to reduce the government contribution from 1.5 cents per barrel to half a cent. This reduced the government contribution from a little less than three million dollars to a little more than half a million.

The second project of OPEC on behalf of the producers was a much harder nut to crack; it was carried on for a long time and the results were not as impressive. As was mentioned above, the government share was 50% of the profits. At the same OPEC Conference it was decided that the royalty payments be considered a production expense and the profits should be calculated after deducting the royalties.[2]

Since the relations between Saudi Arabia and the Arabian American Oil Company (Aramco) and the relations between Iran and the Iranian International Consortium were on a very friendly basis, the two governments were requested to open negotiations for expensing royalties. The companies stubbornly refused to yield and insisted on the maintenance of the existing payment structure. The negotiations moved from one place to another, and at the end all producers participated.

The negotiations were carried on for two years. At the end all parties agreed—except Iraq—on a compromise solution submitted by the companies, for a period of three years. The companies would recognize, in principle, the royalties as expenses, but since they were selling their oil to their customers at discounts from the posted prices, they were to be allowed to deduct from the posted prices 8½% in the first year, 7½% in the second year and 6½% in the third year. In order to consider 1964 the first year of the agreement, a special OPEC conference was convened at Geneva in December to approve the arrangement. At the end of the month OPEC announced that five Middle Eastern countries—except Iraq—approved the formula. Oil specialists estimated that as a result of the formula, the producing countries earned an average additional 3.5 cents per barrel of oil for the first year, 4 cents for the second year and 4.5 cents for the third year. These increases were reflected in the producers' income.

However, the main objective for which OPEC was organized—the restoration of the price cuts—was not attained. It should be noted

(2) Assuming that profits were $4 per barrel, the governments share would be $2, 50 cents as royalty, and the balance of $1.50 would have made up 50% of the profits. But if the royalties were expensed, the government would receive 50 cents, and from the balance of $3.50 it would receive $1.75 as the 50% of the profits, making a total of $2.25 instead of the previous total of $2.

that from the very beginning of the establishment of OPEC Venezuela and the Middle Eastern producing countries differed as to methods of achieving their aims. The former was interested in regulating production in order to raise prices, the latter were primarily interested in restoring the price cuts and were not concerned with regulating production. On the contrary, they were interested in increasing production of oil in order to augment their revenue.

In spite of the efforts of Venezuela to convince the Middle Eastern producers of the benefits in regulating production, they were not convinced. But after five years of unsuccessful efforts OPEC tried, at its ninth conference which met in 1965 in Tripoli, Lebanon, to control production. However, the major difficulty was to find an acceptable base for regulating production. Iran, which had the biggest population in the Middle East, demanded that the base be population; Saudi Arabia and Kuwait, which had the largest oil reserves, demanded that the base be reserves. Each group promoted its own advantage as the base, and no common base to which all would agree could be found. In fact, the organization never attempted to cut production, it merely attempted to limit the increased rate of production.

In 1965 OPEC decided that during the coming year producers should limit themselves to the following schedule of increases over 1965; Kuwait 5%, Qatar 6%, Saudi Arabia 9%, Iraq 9% and Iran 16%. However, the producers did not abide by the schedule, and the organization was powerless to enforce the rates. On February 14, 1966, the Saudi Arabian Oil Minister, Ahmad Zaki al-Yamani, declared that his government did not accept the OPEC decision to control crude oil production in his country. The actual percentage increases in production in 1966 were: Iran 11%, Iraq 6%, Kuwait 5%, Qatar 25% and Saudi Arabia 18%. The rate of growth for the entire Middle East was 12% over 1965, while the average increase for the period 1961/65 was 10.5%. From then until 1973 OPEC did not try to regulate production.

In June 1967 the Six Day War broke out. It brought about changes which affected the development of the oil industry in the region. The revolutionary changes which took place in the years that followed the war affected the relations between the producers and the companies, the relations between the Great Powers and the relations between the producing countries and the consuming countries.

2 From the Six Day War to the End of 1970

Right after the outbreak of the Six Day War the representatives of the Arab oil producing and transporting countries met on June 4-5 and decided to stop the flow of oil to world markets and prevent Arab oil from reaching directly or indirectly any country which supported or was obligated to support Israel. On June 6, Syria announced that she had closed all the pipelines from Iraq and Saudi Arabia which crossed her territory. On the same day Lebanon announced that she had banned the loading of Iraqi and Saudi Arabian oil in tankers at the terminals in her territory. On the following day Saudi Arabia announced that she had banned the loading of tankers bound for countries which supported Israel, and prohibited export of oil.

This development of instituting an oil boycott against consuming countries because of political considerations was a radical innovation in the history of the modern Arab movement. For from the very moment that the Arab League leaders realized the international importance of the Middle East oil they tried to involve it in the Arab political struggle. But the major Arab oil producers, Saudi Arabia and Iraq, steadfastly and persistently refused to permit their oil, which they considered their own economic resource, to become a political weapon of the Arab movement. However, after the Qassem revolt in Iraq the Arab League leaders succeeded, with the aid of Iraq, in organizing in 1959 the Arab Petroleum Congress. The aims of the Congress were limited and far from revolutionary. Six congresses were held between 1959 and June 1967. They served primarily as a propaganda platform for the Arab movement. The Arab oil producers still refused to permit the Arab League to gain control of their oil. The Congress had no executive power and no permanent organization; it had no means of enforcing its decisions.

However, the outbreak of the war in June 1967 had emotionally swept the Arab world, and in the electrified atmosphere the major producers gave up, for a while, their persistent stand and adopted the above mentioned measures. But the negative economic consequences of those measures were soon apparent and the producers rushed to revoke them. Less than a week after Saudi Arabia prohibited the export of oil, the government permitted Aramco to renew its normal operations, to load tankers, except those whose destination was the United States and Great Britain. Kuwait resumed her oil exports on June 14, Iraq on the 15th and Libya on July 5.

For it became clear to all producers, after calmer tempers prevailed, that they suffered more from the boycott than the Western countries against whom it was aimed. In July the Saudi Arabian Oil Minister announced that as a result of the boycott his government's oil revenue was seriously reduced, and it was necessary to cancel a number of economic development projects and to impose, temporarily, certain taxes.

With Saudi Arabia as a spokesman, the major producers began at the end of June to call for the revocation of the boycott. Algeria accused Saudi Arabia of permitting her oil to reach countries which supported Israel, and expressed grave doubts if Kuwait ever enforced the boycott. Libya openly demanded the calling off of the embargo because it did not affect the European countries, for they obtained their oil from other Arab countries.

The difference of opinion about the oil boycott reflected the inter-Arab antagonisms of the period. At the meeting of the Arab foreign ministers which took place early in August 1967 at Khartoum, Iraq presented an economic war plan against the Western countries which included an oil embargo. When the oil, finance and economy ministers met in the middle of the month in Baghdad and discussed the plan the inter-Arab discord emerged. Iraq, Algeria, Egypt and Syria supported the plan, Saudi Arabia, Kuwait, Libya, Jordan, Morocco and Tunisia opposed it. Unable to arrive at a decision, it was decided to deal with it at the end of the month at the foreign ministers meeting which was to prepare for the Summit conference. At that meeting Saudi Arabia declared that she would not stop the operation of the oil industry, Libya opposed the oil boycott and both were supported by Kuwait. All three stressed the fact that their economies depended on the oil revenue, and without it their economic structures might collapse.

At the Summit conference at Khartoum in August-September, the major oil producers carried on behind-the-scenes negotiations with Egypt for the terms of an official calling-off of the oil boycott. Egypt demanded compensation for the war losses to her economy. At a plenary meeting of the conference President Gamal Abdel Nasser urged the oil-producing countries to grant aid to the victims of the war, for which he would not object to the lifting of the oil boycott. After calculating the war losses of Egypt and Jordan, as the countries which suffered most from the war, and after obtaining the consent of the major oil producers to an annual compensation of $135 million, the conference agreed to call off the boycott. The resolution to that effect stated that the conference "decided to resume the pumping of oil, since oil is a positive Arab resource that can be used in the service of Arab goals".

The hasty oil boycott pointed up to the three major oil producers —Saudi Arabia, Kuwait and Libya—the danger to their very existence that lurked when their oil was used for political purposes. *Al-Ahram*, of September 8, 1967, made the point that if the boycott had continued the Arab oil producers would have lost their world oil markets forever, and that Saudi Arabia and Libya would have suffered from unemployment. Representatives of the three producers, therefore, met in Beirut in January 1968 and decided to establish the Organization of Arab Petroleum Exporting Countries (OAPEC), whose basic objective was protection of the economic character of the oil. Membership requirements in the new organization were: the applying country must be Arab, its major export must be oil, and all the three founding members must vote favorably on the application. These requirements ruled out Algeria and Egypt and eliminated all the other members of the Arab League. Iraq did qualify but at the time was not interested in joining. Because of her radical orientation, she would not—had she applied—have obtained the vote of the three conservative founding members. The three major producers aimed at securing themselves against being swept again by high emotional fever, endangering their oil in the Arab political struggle.

The inter-Arab relationship pattern of OAPEC was clear. Until the Qassem revolution, Iraq was in the conservative camp and resisted, with Saudi Arabia, Arab League efforts of utilizing oil for political purposes. After the revolution, as mentioned above, Iraq was the initiator in organizing the Arab Petroleum Congress; and in spite of her very serious differences with Egypt, she remained in the radical group of the League. After the hasty decision to institute the oil boycott the major producers realized that they paid heavily for their mistake, not only in loss of revenue during the boycott, but also in heavy yearly payments to Egypt and Jordan thereafter. They therefore banded together to protect their economic interests from the radical members of the League.

The impact of the oil boycott on the European oil supply system was very light, for the boycott lasted a very short time. But the closure of the Suez Canal after the war created a transportation crisis. Oil from Libya and parts of Saudi Arabia and Iraq flowed in pipelines, but the rest of the Middle East oil had to be shipped around Africa. But because of the lessons learned from the first closure of the Suez Canal in 1956, the European countries managed to utilize their stock-piled oil until the new oil which had sailed around Africa began to arrive.

The method of supplying Western Europe with oil in times of emergency also underwent a basic change. In the first Suez crisis, the United States rushed to the aid of Western Europe and organized the Middle East Emergency Committee which successfully supplied oil until the Canal was reopened and the regular supply restored. But in this generous and helpful move was a very bitter pill for the Western European countries. It placed them on an absolute dependence, even though on an emergency basis, on the United States, a prospect they did not relish; and they had to pay for their oil with American dollars, which put a heavy strain on their monetary resources. When the crisis was over, all the Western European countries adopted measures which would free them from dependence on the United States. When the second Suez Canal crisis came along they were in no need of the United States' help, although the latter proffered it.

Nevertheless, the 1967 war and the consequent developments became new factors in the relations between the producers and the companies. The demand for oil began to rise while production decreased because of the Suez Canal closure and sabotage of the pipelines. In Iraq for instance, production in 1967 was 15% lower than in 1966, and the total Middle East share in world production, which was steadily rising, remained the same in 1967 as it was in 1966. The decline in the production rate encouraged OPEC to continue with its efforts.

The two major items on the agenda of the OPEC 13th conference, which met in Rome in the middle of September 1967, were the posted prices of Libyan oil and of Iraqi oil which flowed through the pipelines to the Mediterranean. Since the oil which went around Africa cost more because of transportation, the two countries demanded a special premium for the Mediterranean oil. The second item was the question of expensing royalty payments. As mentioned in the previous chapter, the royalty expensing issue had been solved for a period of three years, and the third year had come to an end.

Two days before the opening of the OPEC extraordinary conference, which was to convene early in January 1968 to deal with the royalty issue, it became known that the companies offered a new formula: 5½% discount from the posted price for the year 1968; 4½% for 1969; 3½% for 1970; and 2% for 1971—thenceforth the full price. All the producers, except Iraq, accepted the formula.

Saudi Arabia and the Arabian American Oil Company (Aramco) reached the agreement at the end of 1967 that the company would not discount the posted price of the oil that flowed through the pipeline to the Mediterranean. The Iraq Petroleum Company agreed to pay seven extra cents per barrel for the oil that came from Mosul and Kirkuk beginning as of May 31, 1968 until the reopening of the Suez Canal. For the oil which flowed from June 1967 to May 1968 the company paid a lump sum of £ 10 million.

It should be noted that although the basic payment to the producers remained 50% of the companies' profits, the change of reckoning royalties as expenses, the elimination of the promotion allowances and the extra payments for the Mediterranean oil increased substantially the payments to the producers. The total direct payments in 1963 amounted to $1,861 million. They reached $3,370 in 1968, an increase of over 180% while the increase in production was only 165%.

When Abd al-Karim Qassem came to power in Iraq in July 1958 tension developed between Iraq and the company. To be sure, right after the outbreak of the revolution, Qassem announced, in order to prevent an Anglo-American invasion of Iraq, that he would honor the Iraq Petroleum Company's concessions. But as the economic and financial situation in Iraq worsened, Qassem looked to the oil company as the best and surest source for increasing government revenue. The struggle between the government and the company involved many issues, but the major one centered on the relinquishment of the non-exploited areas of the concessions.

Since 1938 the oil concessions of the Iraq Petroleum Company and its subsidiaries, the Mosul and Basrah oil companies, extended over the entire territory of Iraq. One of the frequent charges of the government of Iraq was that the company curtailed oil production and development while the Iranian Company constantly expanded its operations. It maintained that the only way to increase production and revenue was for the company to relinquish parts of the concession areas, which would be granted to other companies for development.

The relinquishment bargaining story between the company and Qassem demonstrated the relative strength and positions of the two. At the end of 1959 the company was ready to relinquish 90,000 square kilometres of its concession areas. Qassem refused the offer and asked for 60% of the areas. However, when the company acceded to the percentage, Qassem reneged and demanded all the concession areas except the parts actually worked. The company refused and the government enacted law 80 of December 11, 1961, which expropriated about 99.5% of the concession areas, including the North Rumaila oil field which was drilled and discovered by the Basrah Oil Company but not worked. All the efforts of the company to modify and soften the harsh provisions of law 80 failed. The Iraq National Oil Company (INOC) took over the expropriated areas and tried to develop the Iraq oil resources and especially the North Rumaila field.

The outstanding aspect in the controversy was the utter helplessness of the Company. France, one of the partners of the company, attempted to obtain a concession to exploit the expropriated North Rumaila field, and she was ready to pay a high price and even an arms bribe for the concession. After some hesitation about her ability to operate the field but with encouragement and technical and financial aid from the Soviet Union and the other members of the Communist bloc, Iraq decided to develop the North Rumaila field.

1970 was the decisive year in the changed relations between the companies and the producing countries, and the major actor in the drama was Libya. On September 1, 1969 a military group headed by Colonel Muammar Qaddafi staged a coup d'etat, deposed King Idris and proclaimed a republican regime. The government was centered in the Revolutionary Command Council headed by Qaddafi who was chairman of the Council as well as head of government; his second in command was major Abdel Salam Jallud. The revolution brought about changes in the governmental structure, in inter-Arab relations, and especially in the relations between the oil producing countries. The trio which organized OAPEC was irreparably damaged, for Libya moved from the conservative to the radical grouping.

As in the other radical producing countries, the revolutionary leaders attacked the foreign companies and demanded higher oil payments and other concessions. Libya argued that two factors entitled her to higher posted prices: 1) her nearness to Europe reduced transportation costs in comparison with the transportation of Persian Gulf oil around Africa (Libya did receive an 8 cents per barrel increase, but it was not enough); 2) the quality of her oil was superior to that of Persian Gulf oil. She demanded a 50 cent per barrel increase. The leaders of the Revolutionary Command Council changed the negotiating tactics; instead of inviting all the companies—22, among them American, British, Dutch, French and German—presenting the government demands, they invited each company separately and asked for the increase in the posted price and other concessions. However, all the companies rejected the government demands. After four months of fruitless efforts, the Command Council named a special negotiating committee. The government announced that the companies offered a 10 cent per barrel increase, which according to the chairman of the negotiating committee would have added $120 million to the annual oil revenue, but the Council rejected the offer.

As a counter-move to government pressure the companies reduced their prospecting efforts by 50%. The government thereupon warned them to continue with full prospecting programs in accordance with the terms of the agreements or they would lose their concessions. At the same time, the radical countries—Algeria, Iraq and Libya—tried to form a united front in their struggle with the companies.

As the demands from the companies yielded no response, the government ordered the American Occidental oil company to reduce the daily oil output of 880,000 barrels by about 400,000. This move was officially explained as a conservation measure. But the Egyptian press reported that the government move was the first step of a plan to affect American interests in Libya. The various companies produced in Libya about 150 million tons of oil a year, 66% of which was produced by American companies. However, what neither the Egyptian nor the Libyan press reported was the fact that 95% of the American companies' oil exports went to Europe; very little of Libyan oil moved to the United States. At the end of June the Government ordered two more American companies to cut their production by 2/3. The negotiations between the companies and the government were broken off.

In the middle of August the government named Major Jallud, one of the strong men in the Command Council, to the chairmanship of the negotiating committee, and he achieved a breakthrough. On September 4, it was reported from Los Angeles that Occidental had reached agreement with Libya on the questions of the increase in the posted price and additional retroactive payments for the period from 1965. As of September 2, production was restored to its previous level.

On September 22, Jallud announced that he stopped the negotiations with the companies; the agreement reached with Occidental would serve as the model for all the other companies to accept without any modifications. The basic terms of the agreement were: an immediate increase in posted prices of 30 cents per barrel of crude oil, with an additional annual 2 cent increase reaching 40 cents in 1975 and a lump sum payment for the differences in prices since 1965. The smaller independent companies accepted the terms, but the international companies which had concessions in other parts of the region refused, at first, to submit to the new terms. However, under the concerted pressure of the Libyan government and the urging of the United States, they agreed. By the middle of October, all the foreign companies operating in Libya accepted the new terms effective as of September 1, 1970. Jallud stated that the new terms would yield the government a total of about $800 million annually. In spite of the new arrangements, the government did not permit the other companies to restore their production cuts.[1]

(1) At the end of 1970 it was reported that the Iraq Petroleum Company would increase the Mediterranean "premium" which it was paying, ever since the closure of the Suez Canal, for the oil exported from the northern fields from 7 to 13 cents per barrel.

As we shall see in the next chapter the Libyan achievements contributed directly and indirectly to the very impressive and decisive results of the February 14, 1971 Teheran agreement and the fateful developments which followed that agreement. The question arises here: why did the companies, especially the international ones give in to the Libyan demands? Had the producers already gained the upper hand over the companies, thereby leaving the latter no alternative but to submit? Or, were there other factors? Practically all oil specialists agreed that the demand for oil had increased after the 1967 war, but not in such proportions as to leave the companies no choice. Moreover, the companies had at their command all the economic resources which could enable them to oppose the Libyan rulers and refuse their demands. The Libyans would have had no choice but to continue with the production of oil under the old conditions. But the State Department interfered in the negotiations and urged the American companies to accept the Libyan demands. Why? Did the United States have political objectives? Was this submission of the companies to bring Libya closer to the Western camp? Or were there other even more mundane considerations?

A State Department representative reported that during the long negotiations between the Revolutionary Command Council and the Oil Companies, a top officer of a major oil company urged the American government to dare the Libyans to nationalize the oil industry; if they did, the Europeans would be told to tighten their belts, while Libya "would be forced to yield soon because it could not dispose of its oil". The State Department, however, disagreed with this approach, not because of its unsound reasoning, but because it was convinced that the Europeans would have made their own deals with Libya; they would have paid the higher taxes Libya demanded and then "the Anglo-Saxon oil companies' sojourn in Libya would have ended". It became clear to the State Department "that a threat to withhold oil could now be effectively employed to produce higher prices". As a result the State Department became deeply involved consulting with the companies "and holding frequent meetings with the Libyans in particular". He reported that the Department urged the companies to comply with Libya's demands. To emphasize the importance of supplying oil to the Europeans and not allowing them to obtain oil directly from Libya he quoted a European Minister who said in 1967: "American companies brutally conquered our market; if they do not keep us supplied at all times, they will be expelled".[2]

(2) James E. Akins, "The Oil Crisis: This Time the Wolf if Here," *Foreign Affairs*, LI, 462-490, April, 1973. A similar analysis was presented by Wilson Lairds, Director, Division of Oil and Gas, Interior Department, in a background discussion with the Senate in July 1970.

From this development arises the question as to the role of the oil companies. We know what their role was in the past; they possessed the technical know-how, they had the financial resources, they owned the means of transporting the oil, they had the international markets, they controlled the industry and determined the price of oil. However, after the producers began to gain control of the situation, raised prices —even before 1970—and increased their share in the profits, what were the special services which the companies rendered the oil consumers?

Professor Morris A. Adelman of the Massachusetts Institute of Technology was of the opinion that the companies could have held out against the Libyan demands, and declared that without United States "active support OPEC might never have achieved much". He stated that when the first Libyan cutbacks "were decreed, the United States could have easily convened the oil companies to work out an insurance scheme whereby" oil could have been supplied from another source. Had that been done, "some or most companies might have shut down, but the Libyan government would have faced a loss of production income". OPEC unity, he felt, would have been severely tested at a time when the producers were unprepared for conflict. The revenue losses to Libya would have been gains to all others, and all would have "realized the danger of trying to pressure the consuming countries."

Now that the companies surrendered, Adelman was of the opinion, and he quoted the chairman of British Petroleum that the companies were serving as tax-collecting agents for the producing countries which they have imposed on the consumers, and that the latter have no say in the determination of the price. Professor Adelman argued that there was no free market between the producers and consumers. A way must be found of reducing the power of the private companies. For the consuming countries "the most important move is direct dealing with producing countries to achieve special low prices". This could be obtained by direct dealing between the producers and the consumers by way of national oil companies of consuming countries.[3] This will create a fair basis for economic bargaining. The producing countries would no longer depend on the international companies for the marketing of their oil, and the national companies of the consumer countries could work out a reasonable price which would be acceptable to both sides. A mutual inter-dependence would emerge: the producers on the consumer national companies for the marketing of the oil, and the consuming countries on the producers for the supply of the oil.

(3) A. M. Adelman, *The World Petroleum Market*, (Baltimore, 1973), Chapter VIII.

In the great and long struggle between the oil producers and the companies and between the great powers, the third element—the consumers—was totally ignored and they had no influence on the determination of prices. The price structure was from the very beginning artificially maintained and determined by cartel practices, at first by the oil companies and later by the producing countries. The consumers were never given the opportunity to deal directly with the producers on the basis of free competition.

The OPEC report for the twentieth conference in Algiers in June 1970, declared that that year marked a turning point in the history of the oil industry. It witnessed major shifts in the price structure and in the bargaining position between the governments and companies. According to OPEC, economic and political forces had changed the international buyers' market to a sellers' market.

As regards production, OPEC noted two immediate factors which affected the situation: Libya's curtailment of production and the closure of Tapline. These two events seriously reduced the oil supply to Europe from the Mediterranean sources, the consequence of which was an increase in posted prices for all Middle Eastern producing countries.[4]

(4) On May 3, 1970, Tapline was sabotaged in the Golan Heights and the Syrian government did not permit the line to be repaired until January 29, 1971. The line which had an annual capacity of 25 million tons, shipped only 8.5 million tons in 1970, from January to the end of April.

3   From the Teheran 1971 Agreement to the October 1973 War

Libya's success in increasing the posted prices and in cutting production, and the decrease in Saudi Arabian production because of the sabotage of Tapline, encouraged the Persian Gulf area producers. At its 21st conference which met in Caracas in the middle of December 1970, OPEC decided to demand a uniform increase in the oil posted prices, a 5% increase in the government share of the profits and total elimination of all discounts which the companies were allowed from the posted price.

All OPEC members, except Indonesia, threatened that if the companies would not comply with the demands they would stop the flow of the oil. The companies were given a 15-day ultimatum to comply, otherwise the producers would take sanctions against them. In addition the "friendly" rulers (by the definition of the United States State Department) sent direct diplomatic messages to the governments of Britain and the United States conveying the same threats. The State Department spokesman explained that if it were merely an economic question or a price issue, the American government would not have interfered; since the threat was to cut off the oil supply, the Department entered into the dispute and performed a public service by preventing the stoppage of the flow of the oil.

President Richard Nixon sent Under-Secretary of State John Irwin, Jr., to the Shah of Iran, King of Saudi Arabia and to the Amir of Kuwait to express the United States Government's grave concern about the threat. The three rulers tried to assure the United States that the threat was against the companies and not against the consuming countries, and that the oil would be made available to consumers even if negotiations with the companies broke down. (They did not explain how this could take place under the existing circumstances.) The Under-Secretary asked for an extension of the time limit of the ultimatum in order to make possible the continuation of the negotiations, and an assurance that agreements reached with the companies would be honored for their full term. On January 16, 1971 the companies submitted a plan for increasing the posted prices and for augmenting the profit share of the government.

The United States Government was not satisfied with its efforts with the rulers of the oil producing countries and the oil companies but convened, on January 20 in Paris, a meeting of the Organization for Economic Cooperation and Development (OECD), to persuade, especially the West European countries, the major Middle East oil consumers, to agree to the increase of the oil price which would make possible the steady and regular supply of oil during the next five years. The following day, the Under-Secretary returned to Teheran and continued with his efforts there.

The result was the February 14, 1971 Teheran agreement between the 22 Western oil companies and the oil producers of the Persian Gulf area. The major terms of the agreement were: Iraq, Iran, Saudi Arabia, Kuwait, Abu Dhabi and Qatar were to receive on the average a 35 cents per barrel increase; in addition the price was to go up on June 1, 1971 and thenceforth on every January 1, until 1975, 5 cents per barrel on each date. In order to meet the inflationary pressures and adjust to the value of the dollar, the producers were to get a 2.5% increase in the posted price on each of the above mentioned dates; all company discounts were to be abolished; and the governments' profit share was to be increased to 55%. The producers, on their side agreed not to seek any further increases or other changes in the terms of the agreement during the next five years. It was estimated at the time, that the new increases in the posted prices and the benefits of the other improved terms would give the Gulf states an extra $1.2 billion in 1971 over 1970 and it would have risen to $3 billion in 1975.

The Teheran agreement was no doubt a very impressive victory for OPEC and inversely a defeat for the companies; although the companies did not assess it as such at the time. As to the reasons for the achievement of the agreement there exists a very serious difference of opinion. All agree that the intervention and efforts of the United States were the immediate causes for bringing about the agreement, however, opinion is divided as to the outcome. Professor Adelman believed that had the American government not intervened and not tried to persuade the companies and consuming countries to submit to the demands of the producers, the latter would have retreated, in spite of their threats. The State Department representative, Akins, on the other hand, maintained that the United States' intervention prevented a grave crisis which would have caused a full stoppage of the oil flow to the consuming countries, especially to the Western European countries and Japan.[1]

(1) James E. Akins gave this assessment of the situation not only to the American public but also to the Arab world. In a talk before the Arab Petroleum Congress meeting in Algiers in June 1972, when the major item on the agenda was Iraq's nationalization of

One thing, however, became clear to all. The producers were not to abide by their obligation not to demand additional increases in the price of oil or changes in the terms of the operation of the industry during the life of the agreement. The achievement of Libyan producers with the aid of the State Department, and the subsequent successful achievement of the Persian Gulf area producers demonstrated to the oil producing countries, on the one hand, their newly gained power, and, on the other hand, the absolute dependence of the consuming countries on the Middle East oil, and their readiness to respond to their—the producers'—demands.

Even before the Teheran agreement was signed, the Libyan government began to press the oil companies operating in its territory. On January 2, 1971 Vice-Premier Jallud met with representatives of the companies and demanded a 5% increase in the government profit share, a special premium for the price of oil because of the closure of the Suez Canal, a certain amount of the companies' profit be assigned for investment in exploration for oil in Libya and for its exploitation after discovery and that oil and natural gas for local consumption be sold at cost price.

The companies attempted to negotiate as a bloc, but the government refused to deal with the representatives of Esso Libya in the name of all the other companies. Unlike the negotiations in Teheran which were on a regional basis, the Libyan Oil Ministry announced on February 16, that the government would not participate in any collective or regional negotiations; it would negotiate directly with the oil companies of Libya. Nevertheless, on February 23 the oil ministers of Libya, Iraq, Algeria and Saudi Arabia met in Tripoli and set up a technical committee to coordinate their governments' demands on prices for oil shipped through Mediterranean ports. They decided that Libya should negotiate with the oil companies in accordance

---

the Iraq Petroleum Company, Akins reported that there were differences of opinion in the United States regarding nationalization. "There are some who say that it would be worthwhile to encourage the exporting countries to nationalize the companies, for the result would be cut-throat competition between the producers and OPEC would disappear. However, we, in the State Department, see the situation differently, and our major concern is security of supplies."

Akins' personality and position had considerable influence on developments in the Middle East. He was Director, Office of Fuels and Energy in the Department of State, and his colleagues said that he was more pro-Arab than the Arabs themselves. After the outbreak of the October 1973 war he arrived in Saudi Arabia as American ambassador, and he immediately began to condemn United States policy in the Middle East. According to State Department sources Akins clashed with Kissinger and he warned the Saudi Arabians not to trust Kissinger. The result of the clash was an announcement in the American press in the middle of August 1975 that Akins was relieved of his post. He left the foreign service and terminated his diplomatic career when only 40 years old.

with the terms agreed upon among themselves. Libya was to inform the other countries of the progress of the negotiations; should the negotiations fail, the oil ministers were to meet again in Tripoli to consult on new measures to be taken against the companies, including stoppage of oil pumping.

However, in spite of the implied threat, the negotiations did not progress. On March 10, the companies received an ultimatum: accept the government demands within 72 hours or face a united front of the four Mediterranean exporters. On the following day, Arab sources reported that the four exporting countries decided to stop the flow of oil should the companies refuse to accept their demands. The two basic issues which held up the negotiations on Libya's part were the demand for an increase of $1.20 per barrel over the existing price of $2.50; and on the companies' part, that the agreement be for a period of five years. In spite of the ultimatum of March 10, the negotiations continued without achieving any tangible results, and on the 28th, the head of the Libyan government, Qaddafi, threatened to nationalize 19 foreign companies, should they refuse to comply with government requests. On April 2, Jallud announced that the government signed agreements with each of the oil companies. They all agreed to increase the posted price by 95 cents per barrel, this amount included 25 cents as a premium for the transportation differential; a seven cents per barrel increase each year, and a 2½% increase annually as compensation against inflation. The government's share in the profits was to be raised to 55% in addition to the payments for the difference in prices during the period 1965-September 1970. The companies also agreed to assign certain amounts of their profits for exploration and other economic projects in Libya. The agreement was for a period of five years. However, on April 24 Jallud told a press conference in Tripoli: "With the September and March agreements we are now receiving the highest revenue per barrel among oil producing countries. It is about $2.15." He pointed out that before the cut in production, under the old arrangement, the government annual income was £ 434 million for about 4 million barrels daily. After the March agreement, the government will receive about £ 778 million for a daily production of 3.1 million barrels. Although the agreement was for a period of five years Jallud declared that the duration of the agreement would depend on the magnitude of investment on the part of the companies in the search for new oil fields and wells.

After the Libyan success, Saudi Arabia and Iraq sought the same conditions for their oil which flowed to the Mediterranean ports. (Algeria meanwhile had nationalized the French oil companies operating in her territory). After prolonged negotiations, the Iraq Petroleum Company agreed on June 7, to increase the posted price by 80 cents per barrel to a total of $3.21; to increase the price annually by 5 cents; and to other conditions similar to the Tripoli terms. The agreement was to be in effect as of March 20. Aramco also agreed to increase the posted price by 81 cents per barrel to a total of $3.18; the other provisions were similar to the agreement between IPC and Iraq, and the effective date of the agreement was to be as of March 20. The three agreements are known as the Tripoli accord.

The impressive and brilliant success of OPEC in the Teheran agreement and Tripoli accord convinced the organization that the time had arrived for widening and extending its objectives and pressing oil companies for further concessions. The first new demand was for the producers' participation in the companies. The request for participation was not altogether new. In 1912 the Anglo-Egyptian Oil fields, a Shell subsidiary, granted the Egyptian government 100,000 "C" shares of £ 1 each, which gave Egypt a 10% limited equity in the company. In the original letter of June 28, 1914 of the Turkish Grand Vizier to the German ambassador granting the Turkish Petroleum Company the concession in the oil resources in the vilayets of Mosul and Baghdad, the Turkish government reserved "to itself the right to determine hereafter its participation" in the concession. In the San Remo Agreement of April 20, 1920 which determined the distribution of the Mandates in the Middle East and the oil apportionment in Mesopotamia it was stated that the residents of Iraq would be given the opportunity to acquire up to 20% of the oil concession. Paragraph 34 of the agreement of the IPC of March 1925 stated that whenever an issue of shares would be offered by the company, Iraqis would be given preference to the extent of at least 20% of such issue. In the original oil concession which Saudi Arabia granted in May 1933 to Standard Oil Company of California it was provided that the concessionary company would make it possible for Saudi Arabian subjects to buy at least 20% of the shares which would be offered to the public. In almost all of the concessions granted after the early 'fifties by the various producing countries to the smaller independent oil companies there were provisions which entitled the governments to acquire between 20% and 50% participation in the companies. However, the question of government participation in the big international companies did not arise until the achievements of the Teheran and Tripoli agreements. The twenty-fourth OPEC conference, which met in Vienna in July 1971, decided to demand, in principle, government participation in the companies. It named a five-member committee composed of the major five producers to prepare a practical plan to be submitted to the next conference which was to meet in September.

The question of participation raised first the extent of its percentage.

A number of OPEC members believed that in view of the general international political situation the time was ripe for cancelling all concessions and transferring the entire oil industry from the companies to the governments. However, the members of the organization were sharply divided on the percentage. Iran, Iraq, Saudi Arabia, Abu Dhabi and Qatar preferred 20%, Libya and Algeria demanded a minimum of 51% or even 100%; while Indonesia, Nigeria and Venezuela —members from outside the Middle East—did not support either group.

The second item on the agenda of the OPEC 25th special conference was the posted prices question. The automatic increase of 5 cents per barrel and 2.5% every year, as mentioned above, were to have been compensation measures against inflation and dollar value. However, the official devaluation of the dollar reopened the price issue. The conference urged the members to enter into negotiations individually or collectively for participation and price increase.

The negotiations which began in October in Teheran moved in November to Vienna but achieved very little. Even the twenty-sixth conference which met in Abu Dhabi early in December produced no results. It was, therefore, decided to meet early in January 1972 in Geneva. On January 20, both sides announced that solutions were agreed upon on both issues. The participation question was too complex for an immediate resolution; the price question was solved by the prompt increase of 8.49% of the posted price by 16 companies operating in the Persian Gulf Area. To stabilize prices the two sides adopted a complicated formula for future contingencies.

The hope of the companies that the Teheran and Tripoli agreements would guarantee price stability for at least five years was dashed in less than a year. They were forced to increase prices in January 1972. However, even the new prices lasted a short time. For on February 12, 1973, the United States devalued the dollar by 11.11%, and the producers began to press for a new increase in prices beyond the formula adopted in January 1972 at Geneva. In April 1973, the companies raised prices in accordance with the Geneva formula, but the producers refused to accept them and demanded a new basis for regulating prices. After dragged-out negotiations under OPEC threats, the two sides agreed, at the beginning of June 1973, to increase prices by 11.9%, and worked out a new formula for raising prices in the future.

But OPEC was not ready to let up the pressure on the companies. The success of Libya in nationalizing her companies (dealt with in Chapter VI) and the huge profits of the Western oil companies prompted OPEC to demand further price increases and to reject the principles of the Teheran agreement that the oil price be based on the inflationary pressures. In September 1973, as the Oil Ministers of OPEC were gathering in Vienna, the Saudi Arabian Oil Minister, Yamani, declared that "the Teheran agreement was dead". The extremists of the OPEC members demanded the complete dismantling of the price structure of the Teheran agreement and that the producers alone determine prices. On September 16 OPEC decided to meet on October 8 in Vienna to work out a new basis for the prices of the oil industry.

The second issue between the companies and the producers was participation. As mentioned above there was a serious difference of opinion among the OPEC members as to the percentage level of participation. Before the 23rd conference in Vienna in July 1971, the Secretary-General of OPEC, Nadhim Pachachi, explained in London that the producers believed that they must enter all the branches of the oil industry, and that this objective was "the most important aim of OPEC". He declared that participation was the means by which the producers would penetrate the oil industry.[2] The 25th conference, as mentioned above, decided that the producers enter into negotiations with the companies on participation.

The representative of Saudi Arabia, Yamani, opened negotiations with the companies in the name of all the Persian Gulf area producers. In January 1972 the two sides reached agreement. In March Yamani reported to the extraordinary conference which convened in Beirut to deal with the participation issue, that Aramco had agreed, in principle, to a minimum of 20% participation. The conference urged all the other companies to follow suit. Later it was reported that the companies operating in Iraq and Kuwait also agreed, in principle, to the Aramco plan.

In spite of the agreements in principle by the companies, the negotiations made no practical progress, and participation became the major issue of the 29th conference which met in Vienna at the end of 1972.

Participation involved a number of aspects. First, of course, was the percentage; second came the basis of payment for the government share, and third, but no less important, was the method of disposing of the share of crude oil to which the government was entitled.

(2) On September 10, 1971 before the meeting of the 25th conference on September 22 in Beirut, Pachachi stated: "The OPEC view is that there is nothing whatsoever in the Teheran agreement or related documents which would prove to be an obstacle to our demand for participation in existing concessions. This demand (participation) is based upon the legal principle of change of circumstances. It in no way falls within the scope of the Teheran agreement which was restricted to two matters: posted prices and the government's financial take."

The conference rejected the companies' proposals, and declared that it was "determined to achieve participation, and in case of failure of negotiations definite concerted action" would be taken by member countries. Yamani, the chief negotiator, warned the companies that the alternative to participation was nationalization, for which the Arab public was ready. By the end of December, Saudi Arabia and Aramco reached agreement for an initial participation of 25%, with a formula of annual increments of 5% from 1978, and 6% in the last year so that by January 1982 it would reach 51%. Compensation for the participation was to be $500 million, with a complicated formula for the sale of the government oil back to the company. Participation was to commence on January 1, 1973. Yamani saw in the participation accord a great victory for OPEC and he declared that it would give the organization great political weight in the balance of world powers. He added tactfully that because the member-states appreciated the power of their weapon they would use it "to build and not to destroy, for peace and not for war, for cooperation and not confrontation".

At first all the Persian Gulf producers—except Iran which had already nationalized her oil industry in 1951, and Bahrain which was not interested in participation—agreed to the Saudi Arabian arrangement pattern. But after Kuwait signed the accord with her companies, her National Assembly refused to rafity the accord, and a number of deputies demanded full nationalization.

The OPEC achievements and victories demonstrated clearly that the era of the producing countries was being ushered in, while the era of the concessionaire companies was rapidly declining and approaching its end. It was obvious that the producers would not be satisfied with their attainments and would press their efforts to gain full control of the oil industry. The oil specialists who were neither oil companies' hirelings nor defenders of the oil producing countries saw clearly the energy crisis approaching and warned the consuming countries about it. The era of the foreign concessions was reaching its end and the era of nationalization was progressing rapidly. However, before we begin to deal with issues which brought on total nationalization of the oil industry in the Middle East, we must return to examine the status and role of OAPEC.

After the Qaddafi rebellion in Libya, the whole structure of OAPEC was undermined, for Libya, one of the founding members switched from the conservative to the radical grouping. The OAPEC conference scheduled for December 1969 in Tripoli was postponed. For the Libyan foreign minister stated at the Rabat conference, although only as his personal opinion, that "oil was a political weapon and must be used against our enemies; it does not make sense to sell oil to America which supplies Phantom planes to Israel, which are aimed to kill Arabs". The pressure from the other countries on OAPEC increased steadily, and in April 1970 Algeria, Bahrain, Qatar, Abu Dhabi and Dubai applied for OAPEC membership. In May they were accepted. Saudi Arabia continued to support the organization for she believed that with the support of Kuwait and the other Persian Gulf area producers she would be able to pursue the original objective of the organization.

In June 1971 the Council of the oil ministers met in Kuwait and a serious dispute developed over the membership application of Iraq. It threatened to break-up the organization. Libya and Algeria sought to include Iraq—her membership would enable the three radical states to dominate the policies of OAPEC—while Saudi Arabia, for this very same reason, sought to keep Iraq out. The smaller Persian Gulf shaikhdoms were standing on the sidelines. Saudi Arabia was adamant. The Saudi Arabian Oil Minister, Yamani, expressed the hope that the organization would "continue to fulfill the goals for which it had been created". The real difference between the two sides, as it was viewed from Beirut, was using Arab oil as a means of pressure to deter the West from supporting Israel as advocated by Libya and Algeria and vigorously opposed by Saudi Arabia, which maintained that the basic purpose of the organization was to keep the oil question out of politics.

However, Saudi Arabia, though at first determined even to break-up the organization, at the end of 1971 had relented. The membership requirements were modified to enable Egypt and Syria to join. Early in March 1972 Iraq, Syria and Egypt became members of OAPEC.

From that day on OAPEC was rapidly converted into an Arab political institution and assumed roles which OPEC could not fulfill. It announced the establishment of an all-Arab tanker fleet, it undertook to build a dry dock in the Persian Gulf and it organized a joint ancillary-service company to service members.[3]

In the middle of June 1972 OAPEC held an emergency meeting in Beirut and resolved to support Iraq's nationalization of the Iraq Petroleum Company. It also recommended that member states extend financial assistance to Iraq and Syria in their difficulties which resulted from nationalization. However, since the organization had no financial resources of its own, Kuwait lent 11.6 million Kuwaiti dinars to Iraq and 1.5 million dinars to Syria.

(3) Dubai withdrew from the organization. The explanation for which was the decision to build the dry dock in Bahrain and not in Dubai.

4   The Producers Develop the Oil Industry

Practically all the producers, from the very moment they fully realized the importance of the oil industry to their future and to the economic potentialities involved, struggled with the concessionary companies for increasing the numbers of their residents in the oil industry. They hoped that in time they would be able to take over the industry from the foreign companies. They also made strenuous efforts to penetrate, slowly but with steadfast determination, the various branches of the industry, and operate them themselves even though at first, on a very small and limited scale.

The concerted effort began to bear fruits in the middle 'fifties—after the producers obtained a 50% share of the profits—when national oil companies were established, and the companies began to relinquish sections of the non-worked areas of the original concessions. The combination of these three factors helped in the steady extension of the role of the producers in the operation of the various branches of the oil and natural gas industries. The tempo of this process was in inverse ratio to the decline of the position of the concessionary companies and in direct ratio to the rise in the position of the producing countries.

The first and pioneering producer in this movement was Iran. The National Iranian Oil Company, known as NIOC, came into being in April 1951 by the oil industry nationalization law, but then its powers and functions were not clearly defined. By the agreement signed in August 1954 between Iran and the international Consortium, which took over the functions of the Anglo-Iranian Oil Company—the original owner of the concession—the industry with its properties and equipment passed into the hands of the national company, which in turn leased them, under specific terms to the Consortium. This agreement assigned to NIOC two direct functions: distribution of oil and natural gas for home consumption, and the operation of the non-basic services of the industry. These included management and maintenance of housing, supply of food and management of the restaurants, medical and sanitary services, technical education of the workers and their welfare services. Since the national company had no financial resources of its own it was assigned certain percentages of the Consortium payments: 29% in 1955 and 25% in 1956; after that year the percentage went rapidly down.

In the middle of 1957 the Majlis (Iranian Parliament) enacted a new law which granted the National Iranian Oil Company wide and broad powers, including exploration for and exploitation of oil throughout Iran—outside the Consortium areas, refining oil, transporting and marketing it in Iran and abroad. As a consequence, NIOC extended its operations and entered into practically all the branches of the industry. It built new oil and natural gas refineries, extended the capacities of the existing ones, and laid pipelines of various lengths and different diameters for crude oil products and natural gas throughout the country, thus creating a great and varied network. It developed the natural gas industry for domestic consumption, for industry and for export. In joint partnerships with foreign companies, it developed a variegated petrochemical industry, and entered the transportation branch of natural gas. It organized many subsidiary companies, each one of which dealt with one of the many branches of the industry.

The national company also pioneered in developing new concession agreements with foreign oil companies—American, Italian, British, French and groups of international oil companies. It granted these companies concessions in areas outside the original Consortium zones, and in the portions relinquished by the Consortium. It developed new concession grants: joint-venture, contractual-service and modified joint-venture. These concession types served later as models for the other producing countries. All the new concessions had the following in common: small areas, short periods of time, and that the foreign company was to organize a new company registered in Iran in which the NIOC was to be partner or full owner, without investing funds of its own and without risking anything in case of failure. The national company was to be entitled to half the profits and to practically all the profits in the contractual service arrangements; the foreign companies were to be subjected to the 50% Iranian income tax on their shares of the profits. All foreign companies obligated themselves to invest substantially huge sums in exploring for oil and in exploiting it after discovery; they were also requested to pay considerable bonuses at the time of signing the agreements, at discovery of oil in commercial quantities and when production reached certain levels. After the lapse of a number of years, the companies were to relinquish the non-worked portions of the concessions, until they were reduced to ¼ of their original grants. The other terms of the concession also favored Iran as compared with the terms of the former concessions. The new companies developed the exploitation of the offshore oil and natural gas resources of Iran.

As an illustration of the advance of the conditions and terms of the new concessions, let us take the first contractual service agreement which NIOC signed in 1966 with the French state group Enterprise de Recherches et d'Activites Petrolieres (ERAP). The French company was to provide capital, technical services and management skills for the expansion of Iranian oil production and its export. ERAP was to lend Iran the money to cover the cost of exploring a 200,000 square kilometre area onshore and a 20,000 square kilometer area offshore. ERAP was to organize a subsidiary Societe Française des Petroles d'Iran (SOFIRAN) under the laws of Iran. At the end of one year SOFIRAN and NIOC were to select smaller areas for intensive exploration. At the end of six years the areas were to be reduced to 5,000 square kilometers on shore and 3,333 square kilometres off shore. When oil in commercial quantities was discovered, NIOC was to set aside 50% of the oil as a national reserve. The other 50% was to be exploited. SOFIRAN was to be only the general contractor, and all the production equipment used by the subsidiary and the oil produced were to belong to NIOC.

The contract was signed for a period of 25 years, and NIOC was to sell to ERAP, during the contract period, 35% to 45% of the oil output of the balance of the 50% at cost plus 2%. From the money to be realized, NIOC was to repay ERAP exploration expenses at the rate of 10 cents per barrel per year until all expenses were recovered. The profits of oil bought by ERAP were to be subject to the Iranian income tax, at the rate of 50%. ERAP also obligated itself to find markets for the oil it was to produce, for quantities of between 3 and 4 million tons annually for a period of ten years. The French company was to invest between $35 and $45 million during the first six years. In case no oil was discovered the French company was to bear all the expenses. Iranian analysts declared that under very favorable circumstances, Iran's share of the profits could be as high as 90%.

The Iranian National Oil Company also penetrated—to be sure with small quantities at first and in certain countries—the international crude oil markets and subsequently also the markets of refined oil and natural gas and products. It attempted to participate in various oil projects in foreign countries, especially in refineries in India and South Africa. Beginning with 1963, NIOC maintained itself and received no funds from the Consortium payments; on the contrary, it was so successful in its operations that it contributed to the government oil revenue. The joint-ventures of NIOC and the foreign companies furnished in 1970 about 10% of oil production and about 5% of government income from oil.

NIOC itself entered the oil production phase of the industry—in small quantities at first—and concluded barter agreements with various countries, especially East European, to supply crude oil in return for services and products. When its own production did not suffice to meet its commitments it received huge quantities of crude oil from the Consortium. During the period 1967-1971, the Consortium supplied NIOC 20 million tons of crude oil annually.

An outstanding accomplishment of the national company was the agreement it signed with the Soviet Union in 1966 to supply 6.2 billion cubic meters of natural gas in 1971, and to increase the quantity to 10.85 billion in 1977. NIOC succeeded in obtaining the huge quantities of gas to comply with the commitment and in building the natural gas trunk pipeline. It was 1,104 kilometers long with a 40/41-inch diameter; it ran from the southern oilfields to Astara on the Soviet Union border in the north. Secondary lines which branched off the trunkline supplied natural gas to many cities and towns in the country, including Teheran. Only one week after the line was completed, at a cost of $750 million, and began to operate on October 1, 1970, Iran signed a new economic agreement with the Soviet Union which provided for the building of a second parallel gas pipeline. In 1971 Iran produced a total of 1,305 billion cubic feet of natural gas; of this, 551.5 billion were consumed in Iran and the balance was exported either raw or liquified.

Perhaps the greatest and most spectacular achievement of Iran in the post-October 1973 oil crisis was the agreement signed in December 1975—after three years of hard bargaining—at Teheran, between the National Iranian Oil Company and Austria, West Germany and France, for the export of up to 13.4 billion cubic meters of natural gas a year through a "transfer arrangement" with the Soviet Union. The natural gas from the Kangan field in the southern part of Iran was to flow in a 1,420-kilometer pipeline to Astara on the Soviet Union border, and from there was to pass in the Soviet Union through Czechoslovakia to the West European countries. The Soviet Union was to take for itself about 2 billion cubic meters of the gas; Germany was to receive 5.5 billion, France 3.66 billion and Austria 1.48 billion. The gas was to be delivered at the Soviet border at the price between 90 cents and $1 per 1,000 cubic feet. The Soviet Union was to charge 63 cents per 1,000 cubic feet as transit fees, making a delivery price of about $1.60 per 1,000 cubic feet of gas in Western Europe.

Payments to Iran, which were to amount to about $5,000 million annually, were to be made 80% in equipment and supplies and 20% in hard cash. Deliveries were to start in 1981, building up to full flow in 1983 and continuing for 20 years. The Iranian part of the project, which was to cost $3 billion, was to be financed 70% by foreign investors and 30% by Iran. The pipeline from the Soviet Union to the West European countries was to be built by a consortium of companies from the three countries. This natural gas deal was considered the greatest undertaking in the world.

The achievements of NIOC were indeed very impressive. When the position of the producers rose as a result of international politics and other factors, the successes of the national company increased. Iran never named a minister of oil, and did not establish an oil ministry: NIOC performed all the functions of an oil ministry. In the middle of 1973, the national company took over, under special conditions, the entire oil industry. (See chapter six.)

The story of the development of the oil industry in Iraq was quite different from that of Iran. Since Iraq had no great refinery of the order of Abadan in Iran, the need for refined products for domestic consumption brought about the development of small local refineries which were placed under the Oil Refineries Administration organized in 1952. This governmental body was given the responsibility for refining crude, maintaining the government refineries and, if necessary, building new ones.

As a result of technical and historical factors, the Iraq Government named various bodies to deal with the different aspects of the oil industry: Council of Oil Administration, General Committee for Oil Affairs, and Oil Refineries Administration. In 1959 the government established the Ministry of Oil and Minerals, and all the other agencies dealing with oil became parts of the ministry. After the government expropriated the Iraq Petroleum Company's concession areas in 1961, as mentioned above, the Ministry of Oil and Minerals was reorganized to encompass all oil activities of the country.

In February 1966 the Iraq government established the Iraq National Oil Company (INOC). The company was empowered to operate all branches of the oil industry except refining and local distribution of oil and oil products, both of which were already operated by established government agencies. The government granted the company 25 million Iraqi dinars, and the company was to give the government 50% of its annual profits. INOC was attached to the Ministry of Oil and Minerals and was subject to government oil policy. The scope of INOC's operations was limited in comparison to the range of NIOC's operations.

During the years 1967-1968 the compass of INOC was expanded to include territory in the areas expropriated from the Iraq Petroleum Company, including the North Rumaila field. Unlike NIOC, the Iraq National Oil Company was forbidden from granting concessions, or even entering into joint-venture partnerships with foreign companies. The national company took over, at first, production operations of Naft Khaneh and Qaiyarah fields, neither of which were of great magnitude. At the end of 1967 it concluded a contractual service agreement with the French Company, ERAP. The general pattern of the agreement was similar to the agreement between Iran and the French company, although some of the specific terms were different.

After the extension of its powers the Iraq National Oil Company faced a difficult decision in the question of the disposal of the North Rumaila field. It was already drilled, and oil was discovered in commercial quantities by the Basrah Petroleum Company, but the field was not developed for operations; it needed transportation, terminal and loading facilities and above all marketing outlets. Should the company undertake to operate the field itself, or should it assign the field to a foreign company? The Compagnie Française des Petroles from which the field was expropriated, though a member of the IPC group with 23.75% interest, submitted to the Iraq Government "certain proposals" regarding the development of the field. By the end of 1967—according to the French Company's annual report—the Iraqi Government had not as yet decided the fate of the oil field. However, early in 1968, not without the encouragement and direct assistance of the Soviet Union, INOC announced that a three-year plan had been worked out to put the field into operation. To obtain the necessary assistance and marketing outlets the company and the Iraq Government concluded a number of agreements with "friendly countries" —so described by the Iraqis—to supply Iraq with financial aid, machinery, equipment and technical expertise to activate the North Rumaila field. In return Iraq was to supply these "friendly countries" with quantities of crude oil. On April 7, 1972 the commissioning ceremonies of the operation of the North Rumaila field took place in the presence of the President of the Iraq Republic, Ahmad Hasan al-Bakr, and the President of the Council of Ministers of the Soviet Union, Alexei Kosygin. Regular deliveries of crude oil to the Communist bloc countries from Fao terminal commenced three weeks later.

Iraq, as Iran, succeeded in bringing about the utilization of the natural gas sources in her territory, which at first were mostly flared. During the oil development period part of the natural gas was utilized for the operation of the oil industry itself, then also for domestic consumption and later for industrial use and even for liquefaction. But by the time Iraq nationalized the Iraq Petroleum Company the petrochemical industry was still in its infancy. After the 1973 crisis she contracted with many foreign companies for the development of great petrochemical complexes running into hundred of millions of dollars. There could be no doubt that the successful achievements of the Iraq National Oil Company were major factors in the decision of the government to nationalize the Iraq Petroleum Company.

In spite of the good and even friendly relations between the Saudi Arabian Government and its major concessionary company, Aramco, Saudi Arabia established a national oil company with the same aims and purposes as the other producers in the region. A royal decree issued in Mecca on November 22, 1962 established the General Petroleum and Minerals Organization, which came to be known as Petromin. Its immediate task was to supervise all oil affairs in the country and it was empowered to enter into any phase of the oil and minerals industries. It had no capitalization and received its budget each year from the government. It was headed by the Minister of Oil and Minerals, and was part of the Ministry of Oil. A Saudi Arabian official source defined the aim of Petromin in 1969, as "participating in different industrial and commercial aspects of oil and minerals so as to establish and develop, in cooperation with private enterprise, oil and mineral industries and industries closely related to this sector". The stress on at least partial participation of private enterprise in the various undertakings was a factor in the financial structure and operations of Petromin.

Petromin organized many companies each of which dealt with one of the various branches of the oil and natural gas industries, and it owned a majority of their stocks; the rest of the stocks were held by Saudi Arabian subjects and foreign investors. Petromin acquired from Aramco the local oil distribution facilities as well as the storage and storage distribution centers. In 1968 Petromin sold a total of 2.5 million gallons of oil products. As in the other oil producing countries of the region, Petromin concentrated on the utilization of the natural gas of the country, except that it had the ground laid out for it by Aramco, which tried to exploit the natural gas for both home consumption and for export. In 1967 Petromin signed contracts with foreign companies for the building of petrochemical complexes, in which it owned 50% of the shares.

In the fifth year of its existence, the national company entered the oil exploration phase in partnership with foreign companies under very favorable conditions. As in Iran, the concessionary company built a large refinery at Ras Tanura on the eastern shore of the country. The western shore area suffered from an oil products shortage. Consequently, the Saudi Arabian Refining Company was organized, in which Petromin owned 75%. This company built a new refinery at Jidda, which began to operate in 1968, and an additional refinery in Riyad.

In order to attain its major objectives Petromin decided to acquire an oil tanker fleet which would enable it to exploit the transportation phase of the industry. To this end Petromin signed agreements with different shipyard companies ordering oil tankers on a barter system, for deliveries of crude oil.

From its many enterprises and activities Petromin gained experience and knowledge in the fields of drilling, refining, and distribution of oil products as well as natural gas and its products, and the petrochemical industry. However, as in Iran, the overwhelming source of the government revenue was derived from the major concessionary company Aramco.

However, after Saudi Arabia had decided on a full takeover of the oil industry and established the Ministry of Industry and Electricity, the government transferred the responsibility for the petroleum, gas and mineral companies and projects from Petromin to the new ministry, and Petromin's functions were restricted to marketing, refining, distribution and transportation.

The fourth great producer in the Middle East, Kuwait, also organized, in 1961, the Kuwait National Petroleum Company (KNPC). It was owned 60% by the government and 40% by Kuwaiti private investors. The powers of KNPC encompassed all oil industry operations at home and abroad. As in the other producing countries, Kuwait's national company's first undertaking was the taking over, from the Kuwait Oil Company, the distribution of all oil products in the country, which the national company received, at first, from the concessionary company. However, after KNPC built its own refinery it marketed its own products. Throughout 1972, its refineries produced 100,000 barrels daily. In 1965 the national company acquired 49% participation in the Spanish group, Hispanoil, and shares in other foreign companies. KNPC took over the areas relinquished by the concessionary company and worked them. It also organized companies each of which dealt with one of the branches of the industry, with the participation of Kuwaiti private investors.

In August 1974 the Kuwait government established a 100% state-owned concern: Kuwait Company for Oil, Gas and Energy. It was to hold the government's 60% share in the Kuwait Oil Company and in the Kuwait National Petroleum Company, together with the state's interests in the petrochemical and gas undertakings. The new company was also to be responsible for marketing the participation crude. In August 1975 when the negotiations for complete nationalization were about to be concluded, the government replaced the new company with the Supervisory and Coordination Committee for Petroleum Industries. The Committee's primary functions were: to form a plan for the oil industry, supervise state oil companies and provide scientific and technical expertise for the industry.

Libya organized a national company in 1970, Abu Dhabi in 1971, and Qatar in 1972. In July 1974 the Qatar company was replaced by the Qatar General Petroleum Company whose responsibility was to supervise and control all state oil interests at home and abroad, including exploration and marketing. The Bahrain National Oil Company —1976.

The pattern of the national company development is similar in all the producing countries. The company begins by taking over the marketing of oil and oil products for local consumption: it penetrates the refining branch, extends into the local transportation phase, expands into exploration and exploitation, and promotes the petrochemical industry. It receives the concessionary relinquished sections and grants them to new foreign companies in the form of joint-ventures or contractual service agreements; and under favorable conditions succeeds to expand and develop the oil and natural gas industries in its territory. It acquires oil tankers and penetrates the international oil transportation field; and finally enters the oil industry in foreign countries.

In comparison with the concessionary companies, the achievements of the national companies were modest and small, but in the process, the natives in each producing country have learned to operate themselves—even though in limited proportions, at first—the very complex oil industry. Thus the importance of the national oil companies was vital in the struggle between the producers and the companies. The experience of the national companies, in combination with other factors, enabled the producers to take strong stands and achieve impressive victories until nationalization, with all its implications, became the major issue between the producers and the companies. By the end of 1975 and early 1976, complete nationalization was being realized.

5 The Transporters

From the point of view of the oil industry, the Middle East forms one solid unit which is divided into two groups of countries. In the center around the Persian Gulf are the producers—Iraq, Iran, Kuwait, Saudi Arabia, Qatar, Bahrain and the other principalities of the Gulf. In this group are located practically most of the oil fields—both on- and off shore. On the fringes of this center is located a second group of countries which served as the transporters of the oil produced to world markets. Without the transportation services of these countries: Jordan (Transjordan), Israel (Palestine), Syria, Lebanon and po- tentially Turkey on land, and Egypt because of the Suez Canal, it would have been rather difficult, if not at first impossible, for the huge quantities of oil produced to have reached efficiently and speedily its world marketing destinations.

The development of the Middle East oil industry was therefore closely dependent, practically from the very beginning, on the rela- tions between the producers and the transporters. Involved were pipelines, terminals, loading facilities and their heavy and complica- ted equipment and, to some extent, refineries. This development consisted of technological, financial and political elements. The two groups of countries complemented one another, but to some extent there was also some overlapping. For although Saudi Arabia and Iraq were primarily producers, long stretches of pipelines were also laid in their territories on the way to the eastern Mediterranean, and thus they also functioned as transporters. Egypt, on the other hand, and recently also Syria, and to a lesser extent Israel and Turkey (when she joined the transporters) were also producers.

Almost from the very moment that Britain and France agreed to develop the Mesopotamian oil resources they discussed the issue of transporting the oil from the wells to an outlet on the Mediterranean either by pipelines or railways. In the concession which Iraq granted to the Iraq Petroleum Company the latter was obligated to build a pipeline of a 3-million ton minimum annual capacity. The question of obtaining the rights to build the pipeline in the territories of five countries—Iraq, Transjordan, Palestine, Lebanon and Syria caused no difficulties. For all of them were international mandates held by either Britain or France. The Iraq Petroleum Company obtained all the transit rights free of charge. Nor did the building of terminals and loading installations encounter any obstacles; the loading fees were very small and insignificant. Problems developed after each one of the transporting countries became independent. Since then, we witnessed an ongoing struggle between the countries through whose territories the pipelines passed and terminals and loading installations built and between the oil companies. After the nationalization of the Iraq Petroleum Company the struggle was transferred to the producing countries and the transporting countries.

The question of building the pipeline from Saudi Arabia to a port on the Mediterranean differed from the building of the first Iraq pipeline, because the Trans-Arabian Pipeline (Tapline) was laid when all the countries involved were independent.

As a result of the Israel-Arab war in 1948-49, Israel ceased, for a time, to function as a transporter, for Iraq closed the southern branch of the pipeline through which oil was flowing to Palestine; and the Iraq Petroleum Company cancelled the additional expanded pipeline which was scheduled to have been completed after the war. As a result of the action taken by Iraq, not only Israel, but also Jordan, ceased to be transporters of Iraqi oil.

Practically throughout the existence of the oil transportation systems in the Middle East, some of the transporting countries interrupted the flow of the oil, sabotaged and confiscated the lines, their equipment and facilities on hand, and periodically closed the Suez Canal for tankers. Continuous negotiations were carried on between the pipeline companies and the transporting countries about transit fees and loading and terminal tolls. After the Suez Canal was closed in 1967 as a result of the Six-Day War, and the rapid development of the super-tanker fleets which sailed around Africa, Israel returned to the transporters group, but in a somewhat different role, and Egypt tried to emulate her.

The fact that the pipelines terminated in Palestine, Lebanon and Syria, refineries—of different capacities—developed in the three countries and in Jordan. The Anglo-Iranian Oil Company and the Royal Dutch-Shell Oil Company built jointly the Haifa Refinery which supplied refined products for local consumption but mainly for export. Smaller refineries were built in Syria, Lebanon and Jordan, mostly by foreign companies, which supplied the local markets.

We may summarize. The Iraq Petroleum Company built parallel pipelines from Iraq which branched off to Lebanon and Syria; the

Trans-Arabian Pipeline was built by the partners of the Arabian American Oil Company from Saudi Arabia through Jordan, Syria and terminated in Lebanon; the Suez Canal served as a very vital passageway for the oil tankers which moved from the Persian Gulf into the Mediterranean to Europe.

Syria

267 miles of the Iraq Petroleum Company's pipeline run through Syria. So long as Syria was under the French Mandate the company paid no transit fees. In 1947 the company began to pay Syria an annual fee of $336,000 for the transit rights of the pipeline and its protection. From then until Januay 1971 almost perpetual negotiations were carried on between the company and the Syrian Government. In 1955, one year before the first Suez crisis, the company agreed to pay Syria a one-time payment of $17 million and $30 million annually in settlement of all past claims. Nevertheless, right after the Suez Canal was blocked Syria sabotaged the pipeline, and the flow of oil was stopped for an extended period. The 1957 revenue from the pipeline was half of what it was in the previous year.

In the meantime, Tapline agreed, as we shall see below, to establish transit payments on the basis of the increased value of the oil after it passed through Syrian territory, Syria therefore demanded from IPC an increase in the transit fees on the same basis. The negotiations between the company and Syria were stalemated. On December 8, 1966, the Government impounded all the movable and immovable assets of IPC in the country until the government's claim for back royalties and higher transit rates had been satisfied. In spite of the strenuous efforts of the Iraq Government, which was caught between the two disputants, to persuade Syria to settle the dispute, the Syrian government stopped on December 12 the flow of Iraqi oil to both terminals: Banias in Syria and Tripoli in Lebanon.

Meanwhile Iraq received no revenue from the oil in her northern fields and was pressing the oil company to settle with Syria or it would have to pay the revenue anyway. The company had no alternative but to submit. Early in March 1967 the company agreed to increase the transit fees by 50% and Syria was to return to the company the impounded property and reopen the pipelines. The new transit fees were to be effective as of January 1, 1966.

Four years later, after a new threat by Syria to shut down the pipelines, IPC raised the transit fees from 14.96 to 22.5 cents per barrel, and an extra ½ cent a barrel as long as the Suez Canal remained closed. The loading tolls at Banias were raised from 3.7 to 4 cents per barrel. The company also undertook to pay a lump sum of $33.6 million in settlement of past claims. It was calculated, at the time, that with a maximum throughput of the pipelines Syria would receive close to $80 million annually from IPC.

After Iraq nationalized the Iraq Petroleum Company the question of transit fees became a serious bone of contention between the two Arab countries. On June 1, 1972 Iraq nationalized the Iraq Petroleum Company (see chapter six) and Syria immediately nationalized the part of the pipeline in her territory. Difficulties were apparently anticipated between the two countries, for while final plans were being worked out in Iraq for the nationalization act, the Iraqi oil minister, Sadoun Hamadi, paid a visit to Damascus late in May and met with President Hafiz al-Asad to discuss Syria's transit and loading payments. According to Iraqi sources the President of Syria expressed the hope that his country would get for the transit rights and loading privileges not less than she received from the foreign company. Later, however, Syria's demand rose constantly, and in the middle of July an Iraqi delegation, headed by the Foreign Minister, arrived in Damascus to deal, among other things, with Syria's transit fees and the Banias loading terminal tolls. But all the arguments the Iraqis advanced, in the name of Arab solidarity, for the cause of nationalization and in view of the financial difficulties which resulted from nationalization, were to no avail. Syria insistently demanded a 100% increase over the fees paid by IPC. The Iraqis expressed willingness to accept any formula or procedure in force between any Arab or foreign state to serve as a basis for a settlement. But Syria was adamant. Resort was made to two Arab oil specialists who were to study the case and submit recommendations. Moreover, Iraq was willing to pay Syria an advance on the transit fees until the issue was resolved; but Syria would not permit the resumption of the flow of oil. Finally in February 1973 a compromise was agreed upon. Syria was to receive a 50% increase over the IPC rate; the agreement was to be for a period of 15 years; but with a right to reopen the payments issue by the end of 1975. Syria was also to buy certain quantities of oil for home consumption at the current price of $3.5 per barrel.

The constant threat of possible sabotage or other means of stopping the flow of the oil by Syria prompted Iraq to seek alternatives to the pipelines running through Syria. In the middle of September 1973 Iraq signed a contract with a group of Italian companies headed by ENI to build a strategic pipeline which would connect the oil fields and the ports in the southern part of the country with the pipeline at Haditha in the north, from which the oil of Kirkuk and Mosul was flowing to the Mediterranean ports of Banias and Tripoli. The length of the line was to be 655 kilometers, and it was to serve a double purpose: to bring the oil from the southern fields, should an emergency arise, to the Mediterranean terminals, or bring the oil from the northern fields, should necessity demand, to the Persian Gulf terminals, hence its name: the strategic pipeline. At the end of 1975 it was reported that the construction of the line was completed.

Iraq was disturbed about the high rate of transit fees she had to pay to Syria and about the low price which Syria paid for the oil she received—the going price was $11.90 per barrel. When therefore negotiations, according to the terms of the agreement, began at the end of 1975, Iraq demanded an increase in the price of the oil in line with the current prices, and a decrease, or at least a freeze in the transit fees. For in view of the great drop in tanker fees, it would be cheaper to ship the oil through the Persian Gulf around Africa than pay the high transit fees for the pipelines. Syria on the other hand insisted on raising the transit rates, at least fourfold, in line with the general increase in prices since the agreement was signed. At the same time she refused to pay the current prices for the oil. At best she would be willing to increase the price to $6 per barrel.

At the end of February 1976 it was reported from Beirut that Iraq had decided to ship the oil from the northern fields through the strategic pipeline to the Fao terminal. She informed her customers, who until then lifted their oil in the Mediterranean ports, that as of April 7 they would have to fill their tankers at Fao.

Meanwhile, to meet the needs of the operation of the Homs refinery, which cannot operate on Syria's oil alone because of the high sulphur content, Syria was importing oil from Saudi Arabia by tankers at the full current posted price. Should Iraq discontinue permanently to ship oil through the Haditha-Banias-Tripoli pipelines the annual losses to Syria may amount $138 million.[1]

The building of a pipeline from Saudi Arabia to a port on the eastern Mediterranean presented problems from the very beginning. In July 1945 the partners of Aramco organized the Trans-Arabian Pipeline Company (Tapline) on the same basis of partnership as in Aramco. The first task was to obtain transit rights through the territories the line would run, and then determine the location of the terminal and the loading facilities. There were several possibilities for the site of the terminal: Haifa, Tripoli and Banias. From the point of view of facilities and availability of technical and technological

(1) The fate of these pipelines may be the same as that of Tapline, for which see below.

manpower Haifa would have been most desirable. However, because of the tension between the Arabs and the Jews the company apparently preferred to have the line run from Transjordan across Syria and Lebanon and terminate on the Levant coast. The company nevertheless tried to play it safe and proceeded with the possibility of Haifa as the terminal. Early in 1946, Sir Alan Cunningham, High Commissioner for Palestine, signed an agreement in Jerusalem with a representative of Tapline which granted the company the right to construct the pipeline across Palestine and locate the terminal at Haifa on the same terms as were granted the IPC in 1931—free of charge. This agreement also covered Transjordan, for at the time Transjordan was still a part of the Palestine mandate. In the meantime Britain granted Transjordan independence, and the company signed a separate agreement with the Transjordan government in August 1946 which granted the company the right to construct and maintain an oil pipeline, in return for a $250,000 annual payment.

Negotiating with Syria and Lebanon proved more difficult because of the tension in the relations between the two Levant countries. Lebanon, anxious to have the terminus on her territory, signed an agreement with the company which granted it the right to construct the line for an annual payment of $180,000. But the Syrian demands were so high that the company threatened to return to Haifa. This threat brought on a diplomatic crisis, not only between Lebanon and Syria but also between the United States and Syria. The American diplomatic representatives were determined to keep the pipeline out of Palestine and divert it to the Levant coast. A compromise was worked out, and on September 1, an agreement was signed between the company representative and the President of Syria. However, the agreement was not submitted to the Syrian Parliament.

Meanwhile tension in the area mounted and finally culminated in the war of the Arab states against the newly created State of Israel. Immediately after the armistice between Israel and Egypt was agreed upon on January 6, 1949, the possibility that Tapline might return to Haifa prompted Syria and Lebanon to compose their differences. At the end of January they signed an agreement providing for the division of the income from Tapline between themselves. In the middle of May Syria signed an agreement with Tapline which provided for the payment of £.0015 per ton of oil moving across Syria. The parent companies of Tapline obligated themselves to supply 200,000 tons of crude oil annually at current world prices for home consumption. The Syrian Government was to take all reasonable measures to protect the property and the employees of the company in return for an annual payment of £40,000.

The construction of the pipeline was completed by the end of

September 1950, and in the middle of November the first oil reached
the terminus at Sidon. The length of the line was 1,040 miles. Part
of the line, from the oil fields to Qaisumah, a distance of about 270
miles, was owned and operated by Aramco; and the stretch from Qaisumah to Sidon and the terminus were owned and operated by Tapline,
which was a non-profit organization. The parent companies bore
the expenses of maintaining the line. When the principle of sharing
profits between the producing countries and the concessionary companies was instituted in the Middle East in the early 'fifties Syria
demanded 50% of the company's profits instead of the per ton basis of
payment. Until the middle 'fifties the company paid Syria for transit
fees an annual average of $1,250,000. Early in 1956 the company
recognized Syria's demand in principle, and in May agreed to become
a profit-making concern and share the profits on an equal basis with
all the governments through whose territories the pipeline ran. It
left it, however, up to the governments concerned to agree on the share
of each in the 50% of the profits.

After long and difficult negotiations it became known that the four
countries: Saudi Arabia, Lebanon, Syria and Jordan, agreed, in
principle, to share equally in the 50% profits. Syria, however, was not
satisfied. At the end of six years of negotiations Tapline signed an
agreement at the end of February 1962 which raised the annual transit
fees to $3,000,000. In addition Tapline was to pay a lump sum of $10
million for settlement of all past claims.

On May 3, 1970 Tapline was sabotaged in the Golan Heights, and
the Syrian Government refused permission to repair the damage. As
a result the pipeline was out of commission until January 29, 1971,
when Syria granted permission to make the necessary repairs, for
which she was granted an annual increase in transit payments from
some $4.5 million to $8.5 million, and a lump sum of $9 million as a
settlement bonus.[2]

Syria as a Producer

In spite of many and varied efforts, at first by the Iraq Petroleum
Company and afterwards by other different smaller companies, no
oil was discovered in Syria until October 1954 when it was found at

(2) In 1968 the flowthrough of Tapline was approximately 23.5 million tons, and the
loading of tankers at Ras Tanura was about 88.5 million tons; in 1970 the flowthrough of
the pipeline was only 8.5 million tons and the loading of tankers at Ras Tanura reached
130 millions. Only in 1972 did the flowthrough of the pipeline attain the 22 million-ton
mark, while the loading at Ras Tanura rose to 225 million tons.

Karatchak, close to the Iraqi border. Three years later another oil-field was discovered at Suwaidiya, some twelve miles from Karatchak. However, the two fields could not be exploited until a pipeline was built to the refinery at Homs for home consumption and to an outlet on the Mediterranean for export. Only in 1968 did oil begin to flow through a 560-kilometer pipeline from the fields to Homs; a 90-kilometer section from Homs took the oil to the terminal at Tartus. Production steadily increased and reached 5.5 million tons in 1973.

Syria did not make public exact figures either about production or about the quantities exported. The government signed contracts with the Soviet Union and with some Western countries to supply certain quantities of oil. But Syria apparently expected to increase both production and exports, for in March 1974 it signed a contract with a Kuwaiti company to expand the daily capacity of the pipeline from 140,000 barrels to 250,000 barrels, or from an annual capacity of 7 million tons to 12.5 million tons. Production increased in 1974 to 6 million tons, and although the government predicted a minimum of 10 million tons in 1975, actual production amounted to 8.1 million tons.

In the middle of July a new oilfield in the northeast started commercial production at an initial rate of 500,000 barrels a day. As a result it was expected that the crude output in 1976 would reach 10.5 million tons.

Late in 1969 the Minister of Oil predicted that by 1973 Syria would produce at the rate of 15 million tons a year, and he claimed that his country's oil income would reach $14.4 million, exclusive of the revenue from IPC and Tapline. However, the major source of oil and income remained—until the 1973 oil crisis—the transit and loading fees; and the major role of Syria remained until that time that of transporter of oil.

Up to the end of 1959 Syria had obtained her refined products from the Lebanese refineries. In 1957 she awarded a contract to a Czechoslovak company to erect an oil refinery at Homs. In June 1959 the 10-million tons capacity refinery was completed; and Syria began to produce oil products from the crude she obtained from IPC and Tapline. The refinery was built for the oil from Iraq and Saudi Arabia which was of a comparatively lower sulphur content than the Syrian oil. Ten years later the refinery began to process, in considerable mixture with the other oils, locally produced crude.

In order to be able to refine the locally produced crude and export products, Syria contracted with Rumania to build a $274 million second refinery at Banias which would refine the heavy Syrian oil. Meanwhile, as mentioned above, Syria—after Iraq stopped the flow of oil through Syria—imported oil from Saudi Arabia in order to operate the refinery.

Lebanon

In spite of concerted efforts during the long period of time since oil was discovered in Iraq, Lebanon has failed to find oil in her territory, and her major role was, and remained until very recently that of transporter. The two pipelines (IPC and Tapline) which pass her territory were the major direct source of oil income, transit and loading fees, employment and other operations.

The first pipeline of the Iraq Petroleum Company, covering 17 miles, was laid free of all transit fees. The terminal of the pipeline was built in Tripoli, and the loading fee was 2 pennies per ton. As mentioned above, in 1947 Lebanon signed an agreement with Tapline; and in the same year IPC agreed to pay Lebanon transit fees amounting £45,000 annually. In 1952 IPC raised the fees to £450,000. A new agreement was also signed with Tapline, raising the transit and loading fees and other allowances.

A long and hard struggle between the Lebanese Government and the Iraq Petroleum Company which began in 1956 came to an end in 1959 when the company agreed to increase the annual fees from about $1 million to $3,458,000. The company also agreed to pay a lump sum of $16.5 million in settlement of past claims. The company obligated itself to raise the output of the Tripoli refinery by 25% and other concessions. Three years later the government signed a new agreement with Tapline which increased the annual payments from $1.2 million to $5.3 million, and the company agreed to pay a lump sum of $12.5 million in settlement of past claims.

In 1967, following an agreement with Syria, IPC agreed to increase the annual transit rates and loading fees, retroactive to January 1, 1966, from about $3 million to about $6 million. In April 1971, Lebanon obtained from Tapline an increase in the annual payments from $5.1 million to $8.6 million, and a supplementary payment of $900,000 when the pipeline reached maximum throughput. Tapline also undertook to pay $9 million in settlement of past claims. After IPC increased the transit and loading fees to Syria in July 1971, it also increased the payments to Lebanon.

When Iraq nationalized IPC in June 1972, and Syria nationalized the IPC pipelines running through her territory, Lebanon faced a very difficult problem. Both because of economic-ideological reasons and unwillingness to tamper with a Western company, Lebanon was not ready to nationalize the pipelines, the loading facilities and the refinery of the Iraq Petroleum Company. However, Iraq would not permit the flow of oil through the Lebanese branch of the line until Lebanon nationalized all the company properties in her territory. In the meantime crude oil for the operation of the Tripoli refinery came by tanker from Abu Dhabi. A special Iraqi delegation arrived in Beirut at the end of 1972 to negotiate with the Lebanese government. Early in March 1973, the government announced that it had decided to take over the pipeline section, the loading facilities and the refinery, for which Iraq permitted 40% of the oil to flow to the Tripoli terminal. The transit and loading fees from the Syrian-Lebanese border to Tripoli were set at 11 cents per barrel. Iraq was to supply Lebanon annually up to 1.5 million tons of crude oil to be refined for local consumption at a price equal to that charged the Homs refinery. The agreement was for a period of 15 years with a proviso that the transit fees and the price of the crude oil be renegotiated at the end of 1975.

In spite of the many increases in transit fees granted by Tapline to Lebanon, the latter asked the company in August 1973 to increase the transit fees and to reduce the price of the crude oil which the company supplied to Lebanon. The company refused to comply with the demands, and the Lebanese government confiscated, from time to time, quantities of oil which came through the pipeline. The relations between the government and the company deteriorated and reached an impasse.

As a result of the international energy crisis Western Europe, Japan and the United States reduced oil consumption. The world demand for oil fell sharply and production in the Middle East was cut. Demand for oil tankers and tanker rates went down heavily, and the tanker industry experienced one of its most severe crises. However, the transit rates for Tapline were being pushed higher and higher while operating expenses of the pipeline were constantly advancing. Tapline, therefore, stopped the shipping of crude through the line at the beginning of February 1975. At first it was believed that the move was technical and temporary, but in April, Tapline announced officially that it closed the line. The reasons given were: the operation of the line caused a loss of over $100 million annually and it was impossible to meet the demands of the Lebanese government.

Under pressure from the Saudi Arabian government the company was shipping limited quantities of crude oil for local consumption in Lebanon and Jordan. On April 26 it was reported that King Khalid ordered the resumption of the operation of Tapline. On the following day a company spokesman stated that the Saudi Arabian government did indeed request the company to supply crude oil to the refineries in Lebanon and Jordan, even should such operation cause losses to the company. He denied however, that the company resumed shipping crude to Lebanon for export. He emphasized that the request of the King was only for a short period of time until the ultimate fate of the pipeline would be decided.

In the middle of May a company representative announced that Tapline could not, for economic considerations, ship small quantities of oil through the line for local needs in Jordan and Lebanon. He declared that the company would not supply Lebanon with any crude, for the Lebanese refinery had storaged supplies which would meet her needs until the middle of summer. Early in July it was reported that Tapline offered to sell the line to Saudi Arabia; it argued that since the line belonged to an American company it would be subject to sabotage either by some terrorist organization or even by some Arab government. Saudi Arabia refused to purchase the line because it would bring her only losses.[3]

The closing of Tapline will cause considerable losses to the three countries through whose territories the pipeline runs. Should the cut in consumption continue, should the tanker crisis persist, should operating expenses of the pipelines increase, and should the transporting countries resist the reduction of transit fees and loading tolls, the pipelines would lose, for the first time in their history, their importance and their role; and oil transportation in the Middle East would become almost exclusively a tanker operation.[4]

In 1940, during World War II, the French High Commissioner for Syria and Lebanon built an emergency refinery at Tripoli under an agreement with the Iraq Petroleum Company. He was to own and operate the refinery during the war emergency, but it was to be turned over to IPC at the end of hostilities in return for the crude oil which the company was to supply. The transfer was duly made early in 1946. Three years later the refinery's quarter of a million-barrel annual capacity was doubled.

In 1955 the Mediterranean Refinery Company (Medreco) built a second refinery at Sidon, 50% of it was owned by Caltex (California-Texas), and 50% by Mobil Oil Corporation (all members in Aramco

(3) The situation became murkier and murkier. By the end of March 1976 Saudi Arabia concluded a 100% takeover of Aramco; nothing was mentioned about the fate of Tapline. Moreover, one month later it was reported that Jordan agreed to pay Tapline $11.50 per barrel of oil instead of the previous price of $3.67 per barrel for the crude which Jordan was drawing from the line. Saudi Arabia was to pay the company $116 million to settle Jordan's outstanding accounts with Tapline and make up the higher price of the crude for the next two years.

(4) See below the discussion of the Elath-Ashkelon pipeline in Israel and the Sumed line in Egypt; the relations between Syria and Iraq have been mentioned above.

and Tapline). The crude oil for the refinery came from Saudi Arabia.

Both refineries were enlarged and expanded over the years. In 1970 the daily throughput of the Tripoli refinery reached 24,000 barrels, and the one in Sidon 16,000 barrels.

Apparently looking for an outlet for its crude as well as an investment possibility, the Saudi Arabian government offered, in the middle of 1969, to build Lebanon a third refinery. At first Lebanon tried to resist the proposal, however, after Saudi Arabia intimated that she might not renew her commercial treaty Lebanon relented. In May 1971, Lebanon signed an agreement with Petromin for the construction of a jointly-owned refinery which would process Saudi Arabian crude. The Saudi Arabian government was to supply the capital, oil and equipment, the last of which it was to obtain from Rumania under a barter agreement. Lebanon's share of the capital investment was to be paid out of her part in future profits.

Early in August 1975, a Lebanese delegation headed by the Minister of Industry and Oil arrived in Saudi Arabia to plead with the Saudi authorities for the delivery of oil through Tapline to the Medreco refinery to meet the needs of local oil products consumption. The closure of the pipeline from Iraq idled the Tripoli refinery, and the closure of the Tapline in February exhausted the supplies of the Medreco refinery. The Saudi King responded by ordering deliveries of 1 million barrels of crude oil via Tapline at the rate of 50,000 barrels a day, pending the conclusion of negotiations between the Lebanese government and Tapline on the issue of the price of the crude oil supplies.

The question of the projected third refinery in Lebanon was broached but it was decided to postpone, for the time being, the negotiations.

Israel

As was mentioned above, the Palestine Mandatory regime granted IPC the right to build a pipeline across the width of Palestine, from Transjordan to Haifa, free of charge. The terminal and tank farm were erected in Acre Bay. An underwater pipeline brought the oil to the loading jetty. The loading fee was first set at 2 pennies per ton; when, later in 1935 a special loading dock was built it was raised to five pennies per ton.

The first pipeline from Iraq was completed in 1934. It ran from

Kirkuk to Haditha; from there bifurcated into two branches: the
northern to Tripoli about 380 miles, and the southern to Haifa, about
470 miles. Immediately after World War II, in October 1946, the
company began building a second parallel pipeline to terminate in
Tripoli and Haifa, but because of the Arab-Israel war the branch to
Haifa stopped at the boundary—42 miles from the terminal. In May
1948, Iraq stopped completely the flow of oil through the existing
pipeline, and Israel ceased to play the role of transporter. The oil
necessary for internal consumption was brought by tanker, mostly
from the western hemisphere.

The consequence of the 1956 Suez crisis was the opening of Elath,
which became the gateway for Israel's oil development. The consequences of the 1967 Arab-Israel war and the second Suez crisis were
the occupation of the Sinai Peninsula and the building of the Elath-
Ashkelon pipeline which restored Israel as an oil transporter. In
1967, two Egyptian Sinai fields produced 50,000 barrels of crude oil
a day. Israel took over the fields and operated, expanded and developed
them. By 1971, some 17 wells off shore and some 100 wells on shore
produced about 6 million tons annually. This quantity was equivalent
to internal consumption. For a few years production reached even
higher levels and Israel exported some oil. However, when Israel
returned the fields to Egypt during the second separation-of-forces
agreement, the Egyptian fields supplied only 60% of Israel's internal
needs.

But the more important consequence of the 1967 war, which resulted
from the closure of the Suez Canal, was the laying of a 162-mile, 42-inch
diameter pipeline from Elath on the Gulf of Aqaba to Ashkelon on
the Mediterranean. The grand design of the pipeline was not a temporary alternative to the long haul of the oil around the Cape of
Good Hope but a permanent resolution of the problem of the mam-
moth tankers which lifted the oil in the Persian Gulf. The new tankers
were not able to pass the Suez Canal even when it was open, nor
were most of European ports capable of receiving the giant tankers.
The new pipeline was offered as a solution to both problems. Elath
port was to be enlarged and expanded to be able to receive the huge
tankers for rapid unloading; the oil would be shipped through the
pipeline to Ashkelon, part would be refined at Ashdod, and from
Ashkelon both crude and products would be shipped in smaller
tankers to the consuming countries. The pipeline company would
also function as a service company and would export oil and refined
products.

On February 15, 1970 the pipeline from Elath to Ashkelon, which
cost $135 million, had been completed. Although the line was original-

ly built by a private company, the Israel government bought out the shares, and the pipeline became a government concern. The initial annual capacity of the line was to have been 12 million tons, with an ultimate flowthrough of 60 million tons. Through the construction of additional pumping stations its original capacity was doubled by July 1970. A secondary 10-mile pipeline brought crude oil to the new Ashdod refinery, which was completed in 1973. Elath port was expanded at a cost of $12 million, to be able to pump through 60 million tons and to accommodate the unloading of the giant tankers.

The major source of crude for the pipeline was Iran. The throughput of the line, in spite of the efforts of the Arab League to dissuade Iran from sending her oil through Israel, reached in 1970 11 million tons; in 1972 it rose to 25.5 million tons, and in 1974 it went down to 2/3 of capacity. In 1975 it went down even more because of the world oil transportation crisis. Early in 1976 it became known that one of the line's major users, Rumania, was to cancel its contract with the line.

The building of the Elath-Ashkelon pipeline, the terminal at Ashkelon and the new refinery at Ashdod presupposed the availability of tankers which would make the disposal of the oil possible. Israel, therefore, steadily increased her tanker fleet. At the end of 1966 Israel's entire tanker fleet consisted of 11 vessels making a total of 330,000 tons; at the end of 1970 it rose to 28 vessels making a total of 1,900,000 tons; and the plans for 1974 called for a fleet capable of transporting the 20 million tons of oil streaming through the pipeline. However, the tanker industry crisis not only stopped the growth of the tanker fleet but actually forced the pipeline company to sell a number of its tankers which were standing idle.

The role of Israel in the Middle East oil industry remained that of transporter. To be sure, in 1955 oil was discovered in Heletz (Huliqat) and its vicinity, but production never reached proportions which would meet even a substantial part of internal consumption. Production reached its peak in 1965 with 205,000 tons, and since then dropped very rapidly to about 40,000 tons in 1973. Proven reserves were estimated that year as 1.5 million barrels. The government and private oil companies have budgeted substantial sums for exploration both on and off shore.

In 1939 the Consolidated Refinery in Haifa, owned equally by the Anglo-Iranian Oil Company and the Shell Oil Company, was completed; it had an annual capacity of one million tons. The crude oil came from the shares of these two companies in IPC. Two years later its capacity was doubled. Because of war needs its capacity was doubled again in 1944. In May 1948 operations at the refinery were halted as Iraq refused to permit the oil to flow to Haifa. By special arrangement with the refinery Israel reactivated it in 1950 with oil imported from overseas, mostly from the Western Hemisphere, and from the Soviet Union by special barter agreements until 1956. Late in 1958 Israel bought the refinery from the two parent owners.

After the Suez crisis in 1956, as mentioned above, Elath became the major port for the unloading of crude oil, and a pipeline was built from Elath to Haifa, which transported the crude imported and the crude produced at Heletz to the refinery. Since local consumption constantly rose, the Haifa refinery was continuously expanded. In 1968 Haifa refined 5 million tons, and of those, 2,300,000 tons were exported. In 1970 the annual capacity was enlarged to 6 million tons.

The Haifa refinery apparently reached its optimum limits of expansion, and the Israel authorities decided to build a second more modern refinery at Ashdod with an initial capacity of 2.7 million tons; it was completed in 1973. Total throughput in both refineries in that year amounted to 6,408,000 tons. In 1974 it was decided to increase the capacity of the two refineries to 13 million tons; Haifa—8.5 million tons, and Ashdod—4.5 million tons.

Jordan

The Iraq Petroleum Company's pipeline ran for 205 miles in Transjordan territory. The company obtained the right for laying the pipeline free of charge, as part of the Palestine mandated territory. The first agreement with Tapline was on the same basis. In between, Transjordan became independent, and the American company signed an agreement with the Transjordan government early in August 1946 which granted the government a transit fee of $250,000 annually, as mentioned above. The agreement was amended in 1952 which granted Jordan $600,000 annually in fees and the crude needed for internal consumption, about 100,000 tons at the lowest of the company's crude prices posted in eastern Mediterranean ports.

After Iraq prohibited the flow of oil through the southern branch of the pipeline IPC cancelled its concession in Jordan in 1963. The only pipeline operating in the country was that of Tapline, which ran about 110 miles in Jordan. In March 1962 Jordan signed a new agreement with Tapline, effective as of November 1961, which raised the annual transit fees to $4 million for the flow of 350,000 barrels daily. Jordan was also to receive a lump sum of $10 million in settlement of all past claims. Four years later, as a result of an adjustment in the boundary between Saudi Arabia and Jordan, the company added $125,000 to the annual payment for the new pipeline mileage in Jordanian territory.

The pipeline was sabotaged in 1970 and 1971 and the flow of oil was interrupted; Jordan's transit income was reduced by a million dollars each year. In March 1971 Tapline again increased the annual transit fees to $7.25 million, and it paid the government $9 million in settlement of all previous claims.

In 1957 the Jordanian Refining Company was organized with a capital of 4 million Jordanian dinars. It obtained a 50-year concession to operate a refinery with an annual capacity of about 300,000 tons. The government was to supply the crude oil which it received from the oil company as part of the transit dues. In 1961 the company built the refinery at Zarqa at a cost of $9.5 million. Part of the cost was contributed by the Jordan government, and the rest was raised by selling shares throughout the Arab world. Crude oil was supplied by Tapline through a 43-kilometer, 8-inch diameter pipeline. In 1970, the refinery's capacity was doubled. In the same year Saudi Arabia offered to remit half of its annual subsidy, granted after the 1967 war, in crude oil.[5]

Late in August 1975 Jordan decided to expand capacity of the Zarqa refinery from 780,000 tons a year to 2,900,000 tons. One year later Jordan signed an agreement with Rumania to build a $500 million refinery at Aqaba with a 6 million-ton a year capacity. The output would be for export.

Egypt

Egypt has been an oil producer since 1911. The production curve was very irregular as the result of the discovery of new oil fields, and the rather rapid exhaustion of the oil fields in a short period of time. Production reached a peak of 2,377,000 tons in 1952, after which a decline set in until 1956 when it was down to 1,729,393 tons. In 1957 the upswing began again until it reached a new peak in 1970 when production rose to 16,400,000 tons, and since then has been declining reaching 7,500,000 tons in 1974.

The history of oil exploitation in Egypt is different from that of the other Middle East oil producing countries. Egypt never granted an exclusive concession to any one company; and a number of companies

(5) See above footnote (2).

always operated in different parts of the country. Through legislation Egypt sought to limit and control the activities of the oil companies, and as a result a number of companies gave up their concessions. However, in the 'fifties the government began to ease the restrictions and a number of the companies returned to Egypt. The general economic policy of President Gamal Abdel Nasser and the 1956 Suez crisis seriously hampered oil exploration. In time a new pattern of concessionary partnership between the companies and the government emerged. The Arab-Israel June 1967 war brought about many changes in the Egyptian oil situation. The Abu Rudais oil fields fell into Israeli hands, but at the same time wide exploration activity was undertaken in the Western desert area and in off shore areas, especially in the Gulf of Suez, and new oil fields were discovered in practically all the areas. One of the most spectacular discoveries in Egypt was the al-Morgan offshore field in the Gulf of Suez. The Egyptians were so impressed with the production magnitude of this field that President Nasser was prompted to declare that in 1970 Egypt would produce 30 million tons of oil, which would provide Egypt with an annual revenue of $280 million. The general manager of the government General Petroleum Corporation went even further by stating that within three years his country's oil revenue might rival that of Saudi Arabia.

Although the huge production figures predicted by President Nasser and others were far from being realized, production continued to expand; new oil and natural gas fields were discovered and oil production in 1970 was three times that of 1967.

After many and varied experimentations in oil concessions and even attempting nationalization, the Egyptian Government came to the conclusion that without extensive and steady exploration throughout the country, oil production would decline. It was also convinced that it could not undertake itself the task of searching for oil. It, therefore, decided early in 1973 to grant exploration and exploitation concessions to many Western oil companies in the various parts of the country which would guarantee increased production. (The experiment of exploring for oil in the Western desert by the Soviet Union ended in failure and the teams left Egypt).

The Government set a goal of an annual oil production of between 375-412 million barrels beginning with 1982, or about 1,000,000 barrels a day. The General Petroleum Corporation prepared a concession form and invited the big foreign oil companies to submit applications for both on shore and off shore areas. The terms were: leasing permits to be granted only to companies registered in Egypt, Egyptians must own 51% of the shares; companies to obligate themselves to invest minimal amounts in exploration for a period of 8 years; they were to pay a bonus at the time of signing the agreement; the development period was to be from 20 to 30 years after the discovery of oil in commercial quantities; the foreign companies were to be entitled to 40% of production to recover their investments; of the balance the Government was to receive 80% and the companies 20%. The exploration areas were generally limited to 10,000 square kilometers, after a stated period the companies were to relinquish the non-exploited areas.

The foreign companies responded to the Egyptian offers and by the end of 1974, the Egyptian government granted contracts to 24 foreign companies, among them American, German, Brazilian, Japanese and others. All of the companies obligated themselves to invest a minimum total of $531 million in exploration and exploitation during the next 8 years. The General Petroleum Corporation received bonuses, at the signing of the contracts, amounting to $66 million. The trend continued in 1975 and 1976.[6]

However, in spite of the overall increase in production—with the ups and downs—the major role of Egypt in the Middle East oil industry was that of transporter through the Suez Canal. The great bulk of the oil coming from the Persian Gulf area—up to 1967—passed through the Canal, and Egypt's oil income was in great measure derived from the transit tolls of the Canal.

After the closure of the Suez Canal in 1967, Egypt ceased to play the role of transporter, and Israel began to build the Elath-Ashkelon pipeline as a part alternative to the Suez Canal, and as an answer to the giant-tanker problem. To counteract the efforts of, and compete with the Israel pipeline, Egypt prepared a plan to build a pipeline parallel to the Canal which would restore her as a major transporter of Middle East oil. In view of the negative attitude of the big international oil companies towards Israel, Egypt was convinced that they would ship their oil through the proposed Egyptian pipeline, and that would bring in important revenue. The Economic Council of the Arab League approved the proposal as an important means of short-circuiting the Israeli pipeline.

The building of the Egyptian pipeline presented a complex of problems, the major one of which was financing it. Egypt would

(6) The General Petroleum Corporation modified its agreement with AMOCO (subsidiary of Standard Oil Company of Indiana) on January 7, 1976. The original agreement was a 50/50 joint-venture undertaking and covered Egypt's major producing fields: al-Morgan, July and Ramadan in the Gulf of Suez and a concession in the Western desert. Effective as of July 1, 1975, under the new arrangements AMOCO will get 40% of production to recover its costs, the balance will be divided during the first two years 83% to the government and 17% to the company; during the following three years 85% to the government and 15% to the company; and thereafter, to the end of the agreement, 87% to the government and 13% to the company.

have to be the owner and builder of the line and would only award contracts to foreign companies. Not being able to finance the project herself she would have to obtain credit from foreign banks. In order to cover the risk of the loans the banks would want to see legally binding commitments from the international oil companies that they would ship their oil through the pipeline. The international oil companies wished to know in advance of their commitments the transit rates which they would be expected to pay, and whether they would be economical. Egypt on her part could not set exact rates in advance.

A French construction company organized a European Consortium which included companies from the major European countries interested in building the pipeline. The length of the line was to be about 210 miles, and the flowthrough capacity about 40 million tons a year. The capacity could be doubled by laying a parallel line; by erecting pumping stations the capacity could be raised to 120 million tons. The Consortium approached the large banks in Europe and asked for loans; the banks demanded as collateral authentic commitments from the international oil companies for quantities up to ¾ of the line's capacity.

In the middle of July 1969, Egypt signed a tentative contract with the Consortium to build the pipeline at a cost of $175 million. France obligated herself to grant Egypt a long-term loan amounting to 25% of the cost in hard currency. Italy, reportedly, was contemplating a similar loan, if Italian companies participated in the project. It was believed at the time that it would take about 2½ years to construct the line. The diameter of the line was to have been 42 inches. The port near Suez was to accommodate tankers of up to 213,000 tons. The pier near Alexandria was to receive tankers from 50,000 to 250,000 tons.

Negotiations continued and a new modified contract was signed at the end of July 1971, in Cairo, for the construction of the Sumed (Suez-Mediterranean) crude oil pipeline. It was to have consisted of two parallel 42-inch diameter pipelines from a receiving terminal at Ain Sukhna, 40 kilometers south of Suez, to a loading terminal at Sidi Krer west of Alexandria. The cost of construction went up to about $300 million. Foreign credits from the participating countries in the Consortium were to be $225 million, $44 million was to be obtained as loans from Middle Eastern countries, and the two major prospecting users of the line, Amoco and Mobil, were to provide $15 million each. The Sumed Pipeline International Consortium (SPIC) was to be managed by a board of directors consisting of representatives of the seven nations whose companies were to build the line.

In between a number of oil companies undertook to ship stated quantities of oil through the planned pipeline. In April 1971 the commitments reached 28 million tons out of a planned capacity of

80 millions. Construction costs were then estimated at $350 million. The negotiations between the Egyptian Government and the Consortium dragged on.

In the middle of 1973 it was reported that American companies attempted to replace the European concerns. An investment company in New York which had been doing business in the Middle East succeeded in interesting the great construction establishment Bechtel of San Francisco in the Egyptian pipeline. Egypt issued an international tender for the building of the pipeline, and the European Consortium and Bechtel submitted bids. Early in October Egypt accepted the Bechtel offer, because it was $18 million lower than that of the Consortium, and decided to award the contract to Bechtel for the sum of $397.6 million. Two American banks: the Import-Export of Washington and Citibank of New York were ready to finance a goodly portion of the project. However, at the end of 1973 Cairo reported that an Arab stock company with a capitalization of $400 million was organized to finance the building of the pipeline. The official Egyptian announcement stated that Egypt would invest $200 million; Saudi Arabia, Kuwait and Abu Dhabi $60 million each, and Qatar $20 million. The company was to issue 40,000 shares of $10,000 each.

Kuwait was ready to invest $200 million but demanded a majority control of the company, which Egypt refused to grant and was, therefore, forced to acquire 50% of the shares herself. But she had to concede to the request of the Arab investors that they be permitted to take out their profits in hard currency.

The project was apparently progressing, and early in 1974 it was announced that Egypt planned the construction of a new refinery at the terminal at Sidi Krer, with a daily throughput capacity of 250,000 barrels. However, early in April it was reported that the contract between Bechtel and Egypt was cancelled, because Egypt refused to pay the difference in cost which had risen in the meantime. Instead Egypt granted the contract to a Consortium of Italian Companies, among them ENI, for the amount of $348 million. But Bechtel was retained as technical adviser and supervisor. The contract provided that the project must be completed in 30 months. The Egyptian press reported that great quantities of heavy steel pipeline had arrived at Alexandria. But no official government announcement was made about the actual construction of the line. By the end of December 1975, *Akhbar al Yaum* reported that the building of the line was about completed, except for the section across the Nile river. This would be finished very shortly and the pipeline would be inaugurated in January 1976.[7]

(7) The London bi-weekly *Petroleum Times*, published an article in the middle of October 1975 about the future of Sumed. The writer was very doubtful about the

When the Suez Canal was reopened, Egypt resumed her old role as oil transporter; but the magnitude of the tanker movement through the canal would of necessity be limited by the level of the transit rate and by the size of the tankers which could pass through the Canal. Should Egypt widen and deepen the Canal in order to enable the giant tankers to pass through it, and she is doing it, the transit tolls would inevitably go up and it would not be economic for the oil companies to ship via the Canal.

In May 1976, the Egyptian Oil Minister Ahmad Hilal told *World Oil* that the pipeline would be completed in December. However, Egypt seems to be hestiating about proceeding with the pipeline program. Some of the government agencies would prefer to devote the available resources for the widening and deepening of the Canal to the building of the parallel pipeline. The National Production Council, responsible for long-range economic planning recommended that the Canal be widened to enable tankers of 300,000 tons to negotiate the Canal instead of spending the resources on the pipeline.

The history of the oil refining industry in Egypt is almost parallel to the history of oil production. In 1913, the Anglo-Egyptian Oilfields erected a refinery at Suez, and since then it had been expanded and enlarged. In 1922, the Egyptian Government built its own hundred-ton daily capacity refinery, also at Suez, to refine the crude oil which it received as royalty. At first the refinery operated only part of the time on native crude and the rest of the time on imported crude. The increase in local production after 1938 restricted the operation of the government refinery to local crude. Since then, the refinery was extended and enlarged. In July 1956 the Societe Egyptienne pour le Raffinage et le Commerce de Petrole completed a third refinery in Alexandria with an annual throughput of 200,000 tons, which could be expanded to 500,000 tons. It began to operate in March 1957. By 1963, the refineries, all state owned, had a total annual throughput capacity of 6,350,000 tons. In the late 'sixties, during the war of attrition between Egypt and Israel across the Suez Canal, the Suez refineries were very heavily damaged. The Alexandria refinery was, therefore, extensively enlarged. After the separation of forces agreement between Israel and Egypt early in 1974, the Suez refineries were rehabilitated.

Because of the quality of some of Egypt's crude oil it was not possible

---

activation of the line. He proposed an epitaph for Sumed: "It seemed a good idea at the time." He did not believe that the great international companies would be interested in using the line, and this for two reasons: security and cost. He concluded by saying, "As the market is at the moment the Sumed pipeline cannot be an economic proposition for the companies."

to refine it at home for local consumption. Egypt therefore exported and imported oil; part of the imported oil was refined and exported.

Turkey

Turkey was perhaps the least important, both from the point of view of production and from the point of view of transportation in the general picture of the oil industry of the region.

In 1948 oil was discovered in Ramandag, some sixty miles from Diarbekr. It was a small field and consisted of six wells. A small refinery was built at Batman. After the change of the regime in 1950 great efforts were made to discover new oil fields. The pattern which emerged and developed was of concessions granted to private companies, government companies and joint partnerships of the two. Oil exploration in Turkey was and is very expensive and generally is not profitable. Many of the great oil companies which obtained concessions and spent huge sums of money on exploration without discovering oil, surrendered their concessions and left Turkey.

New oil fields were discovered in the Sirit province, but they could not be exploited until a pipeline was built early in 1967, from the oil-fields to Dortyol on the Gulf of Iskanderun. The pipeline runs 310 miles, and its diameter is 18 inches, with a flowthrough capacity of 70,000 barrels a day. As a result production in that year increased by 5 million barrels, a 47% increment.

The oil reserves estimates were constantly increasing until 1969, and after that they began to decline until they reached, in 1974, ¼ of the 1964 estimates. Production also began to decline. In 1971 it was only 2/3 of what it was in the previous year. After that it increased. However, in 1974 it was still 2 million barrels below that of 1970.

By its own effort and in partnership with foreign companies the Turkish government erected a number of refineries.

Since 1974 there had been signs that Turkey was about to join the transporters of the region. From time to time, during the oil history of Iraq, plans were advanced for building a pipeline from the northern oil fields across Turkey to a terminal on the Gulf of Iskanderun. The motives for these plans were varied: an alternative to the existing pipelines via Syria which were sabotaged and were inoperative for extended periods, and for additional outlets for greater quantities of oil which the existing lines were incapable of carrying. But many years passed and the plans did not advance to practical application. However, after the frequent sabotage acts since 1968, and the ever increasing demands for higher transit fees, the plans began to advance rapidly. Both the Iraq National Oil Company and the Turkish

National Oil Company, each for its own reasons, began to discuss seriously the plans for the pipeline. By the end of August 1973 an agreement was signed between the two governments for the building of the pipeline which would transport crude oil from the Kirkuk oil fields to a Turkish port. The annual flowthrough of the line was set at 25 million tons with a possibility of raising it to 35 million tons. 40% of the oil was to go to Turkey to meet her own needs, the rest was to be for export. Iraq was to build the part of the line which would run in her territory, and Turkey the part in her territory. The agreement was for a period of 20 years, and Iraq was to pay Turkey 35 cents per barrel transit fees. The cost of building the pipeline was first estimated at $350 million, but was raised later to $400 million. For a while the Turkish Grand National Assembly refused to ratify the agreement. Members expressed fears about the safety of the pipeline which was to pass through Kurdish territory; they also resented the high price which Iraq charged Turkey for the oil. But in November 1974, Iraq signed an agreement with a German construction company for the laying of the pipeline in her territory. The diameter was to be 40 inches and was to be completed in two years at a cost of 60 million Iraqi dinars. A Japanese company was to supply the necessary pipe. Turkey also signed an agreement with a German company for the building of the section of the line in her territory.

It would appear that, in spite of the general bleak outlook for the pipeline industry in the region, Turkey and Iraq will complete the pipeline. Turkey because she needs the oil from Iraq; and Iraq because she is determined to find alternatives to the pipelines running through Syria.

When Iran increased her natural gas output she attempted to find transport facilities to ship gas to a Mediterranean port for transhipment to Europe. Early in September 1974, it was reported that Turkey and Iran signed an agreement in Ankara for the building of a natural gas pipeline from the Iranian gas fields in southern Iran to the Gulf of Iskanderun, a distance of some 1800 kilometers. At the loading port were to be built plants which would compress the gas for shipment to Europe. The cost of building the pipeline and the other terminal facilities was estimated between 6 and 10 billion. In view of the agreement reached between Iran and the Western European countries for the shipment of natural gas via the Soviet Union described in Chapter IV, it would not seem likely that another line would be built.

When the Iraq-Turkey pipeline is completed, and if the Iran-Turkey pipeline is built, Turkey will join the transporters group in the Middle East.

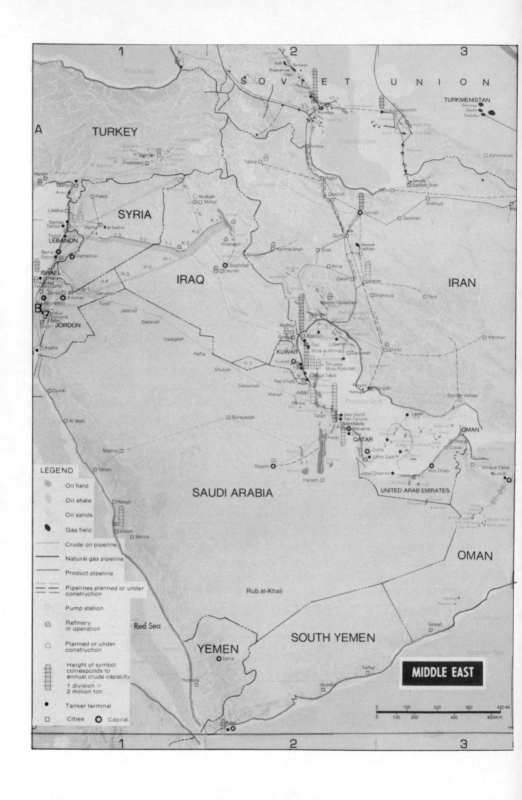

LEGEND

Oil field

Oil shale

Oil sands

Gas field

Crude oil pipeline

Natural gas pipeline

Product pipeline

Pipelines planned or under construction

Pump station

Refinery in operation

Planned or under construction

Height of symbol corresponds to annual crude capacity
1 division = 2 million ton

Tanker terminal

Cities   Capital

MIDDLE EAST

SOVIET UNION

TURKMENISTAN

TURKEY

SYRIA

LEBANON

ISRAEL

JORDON

IRAQ

IRAN

SAUDI ARABIA

KUWAIT

BAHRAIN

QATAR

UNITED ARAB EMIRATES

OMAN

OMAN

Red Sea

Rub al-Khali

YEMEN

SOUTH YEMEN

Persian Gulf

Arabian Sea

6 Nationalization and Participation

In the long struggle of the oil producing countries to obtain a greater share of the revenue from the oil produced by the concessionaire companies it was inevitable that the issue of nationalization should become a major factor in the pattern of relations between the two. However, throughout the period of oil development in the Middle East, nationalization did not loom as a serious threat until the 'seventies. The explanation for this phenomenon was no doubt the disastrous failure of Iran's attempt to nationalize her oil industry in 1951. To be sure, the United States succeeded in finding a solution to the crisis and rescued Iran from total defeat by organizing the international Consortium, which made it possible for the Iranians to agree to continue with the exploitation of the oil by foreign companies, but it was only a face-saving device. The ownership of the facilities of the industry was transferred to the National Iranian Oil Company (NIOC), and it in turn leased all the production and refining facilities to the Consortium. But practically, the attempt of nationalization was a total failure; after a three-year struggle Iran was forced to surrender. Since then, whenever the question of nationalization was brought up the lesson of Iran was recalled and the subject was quickly dropped.

Why did Iran's attempt fail? Why was she forced to accept the United States' solution as the only way out of an impossible situation? The answer to these questions is rather complex. It is to be recalled that the demand for oil in the world was much lower than the supply and there were available alternatives to Iranian oil both in the Middle East and in other oil regions. The international climate made it impossible for a small country like Iran to challenge with impunity first Britain and then also the United States. The world oil markets were in the hands of the international oil companies, they operated as a cartel and did not permit either actual or potential purchasers to buy Iranian nationalized oil. Iran had neither the technological know-how nor the great financial resources necessary to operate the industry by herself; and she was desperately in need of the oil revenue for her daily existence.

The Iranians believed that the United States would side with them in their struggle with the British oil company for two reasons: they would want to gain new oil resources in the Middle East at the expense of the British, and their fear that serious disturbances in Iran resulting from the nationalization struggle would invite Soviet penetration into Iran. But in spite of some of the basic differences between the British and the Americans on the issue of nationalization, they were both determined to protect their common interest, and did not allow Iran to arbitrarily cancel a legal concession without paying proper compensation. Although the United States recognized, in principle, the right of Iran to nationalize the oil industry in her territory and urged Britain to do the same, the United States could not agree with Iran that she was not obligated to pay compensation for the nationalized concession. Moreover, the other concessionaire companies in the Middle East were united in their determination in preventing Iran from attaining her objective, lest they would all face the same fate in their concessions. They were all ready to support the Anglo-Iranian oil company in protecting its legitimate rights.

It should also be pointed out that the jump from 16% to 50% in the share of the producing countries in the profits ushered in a period of prosperity in all the producing countries, and they were not ready to jeopardize their newly won wealth through Iran's nationalization adventure. On the contrary, they exploited the situation by demanding from their companies an increase in production at the expense of Iran.

In the late 'fifties and early 'sixties, when world demand for oil continued to fall and prices were cut, the producing countries were primarily interested in restoring the oil prices to their previous level. To achieve this they set up the Organization of Oil Exporting Countries (OPEC), whose purpose and efforts were the restoration of the price cut. Until the late 'sixties OPEC's endeavors were unsuccessful.

The issue of oil nationalization for the Arab producing countries was even more complex. It involved, in addition to the above factors, the question of utilizing the oil as a political weapon in the Arab general national aim; it entailed psychological factors which stemmed from an inferiority complex *vis-a-vis* the companies and their home governments, and it contained inter-Arab friction and personality conflicts. The leaders of the Arab League tried, ever since they realized the importance of oil in the world economy, to involve the Arab oil with the Arab struggle, but were repeatedly and consistently rebuffed by the great producers. Saudi Arabia and Iraq refused to surrender their oil to the Arab national movement. They viewed their oil as a

national economic asset which must not become embroiled in the
political battles.

The Arab League named an oil committee, but it was actionless
and powerless. However, after the Qassem revolution in Iraq in July
1958, a change took place. Qassem believed that if he were backed
by a united Arab front he could successfully cope in his battle with
the Iraq Petroleum Company. In Saudi Arabia the Amir Faisal rose
to power, and unlike his brother King Saud, recognized the leadership
of the Egyptian president Gamal Abdel Nasser, the dominant element
in the Arab League. At the same time, the general manager of the
Saudi Arabian Oil and Mineral Directorate, Abdullah al-Tariqi, was
strongly advocating very close cooperation among the Arab producing
countries and demanded concessions from the companies.

Iraq, therefore, took the initiative and convened, in April 1959, the
first Arab Petroleum Congress. However, not a single Arab delegate
to the Congress advocated nationalization, nor were any threats made
of modifying the terms of the existing concessions unilaterally by
the producers. At the second Congress which was held in Beirut in
October 1960, al-Tariqi attacked the concessionaire companies and
demanded that they reorganize themselves as integrated companies,
that is from exploration through marketing, in order that the governments receive their 50% share in the profits not only from production
but also from all the other operations. Only after al-Tariqi was relieved of his post in Saudi Arabia and became a private oil-consultant
did he emerge as the firey advocate and agitator of nationalization.

Al-Tariqi's successor as Saudi Arabia's Minister of Oil, Ahmad
Zaki al-Yamani, declared in 1965 that the economic ideology of
Saudi Arabia was based on private enterprise, and his country was,
therefore, opposed to nationalization. But it would seem that in a
country as autocratic as Saudi Arabia, the ideological principle of
private enterprise would hardly be a deterrent for the government
not to nationalize the oil industry. We must, therefore, assume that
other factors deterred the Saudi Arabian government.

An important factor which deterred all the producing countries from
nationalizing the oil industry was the determination of each one of
them to increase oil production even at the expense of the others.
They refused consistently to cooperate in regulating oil production.
Nationalization would inevitably result in cut-throat competition
among the producers and would bring down prices drastically.

Instead, they followed a system of gradual acquisition of the
industry which would enable them to learn and master the industry
in its entirety. The first step was the establishment in each country of
a national oil company, which was initially limited in its functions

and responsibilities. These national companies began by taking over from the concessionaire companies local distribution of oil and oil products. Next came responsibility for refining for local needs, then local transportation, and ending with marketing, very limited to be sure, in foreign countries.

The second step was participation in the concessionaire companies, which were producing concerns. At the beginning the participation demand was modest, and it aimed at penetrating the management of the companies in order to gain knowledge and experience in the administrative aspect of the industry. Slowly but steadily participation was to increase until the producers would acquire a majority holding in the companies and control the industry. But even then they would have wanted the companies to continue to function fully by letting them retain 49% of the holdings, a vested interest in the industry. The increase in the world demand for oil which began in the late 'sixties hastened the requests for participation, but it had to be small, otherwise the producing countries would have risked responsibility for the operation of the industry of which they were incapable.

The efforts and tactics of the producers to obtain participation were discussed in chapter III; here should be added the frank explanations of the motive for participation. Muhammad Joukhdar, deputy governor of Saudi Arabia's Petromin and former Secretary General of OPEC, explained early in August 1971: "It is common knowledge that more than 90 percent of all the oil production is undertaken by companies which are not subject to the principle of participation. It is neither logical nor wise for oil producing countries to allow this situation to continue until the date of expiry of the agreements, with the result that—notwithstanding successive changes in the structure of exploration, drilling and production contracts since the early 'sixties—they would suddenly find themselves responsible for a complex and diverse industry. It would not be possible for them to run this industry with the necessary high standards of competence and technical skill without prior and effective experience in all aspects of the petroleum industry". In short, the purpose of participation was to enable the producers to take over the industry when the companies would leave. "The National interest is to prepare, in an effective manner, for the time when the entire industry will revert to the state".

The Secretary General of OPEC, Nadhim Pachachi, explained the desire for participation in a similar vein when he was interviewed over Radio Denmark after OPEC adopted the participation resolution. He stated that most of the crude oil produced in OPEC countries was covered by concession agreements that were concluded before World War II. Circumstances have drastically changed in the past twenty years. The producing countries, he continued "want to have a direct role in the management of the exploitation of their resources, so as to gain know-how and to develop national expertise in the production and marketing of oil. Remember that sooner or later all the concessions will revert to the state when the concession agreements expire. Oil exporting countries have to prepare themselves for assuming the responsibility for the management of the oil industry when the concession agreements expire". He emphasized that "the main objective of our participation is to gain know-how rather than to increase revenue".

However, when the representatives of the companies and of OPEC gathered in Geneva early in 1972 to deal with the issue of participation, the Secretary-General declared: "Our recent demand for government participation in existing oil concessions is based on our conviction that such direct participation would reinforce and render more effective our right to permanent sovereignty over our resources".

By the end of 1972, as was mentioned above, all the producing countries in the Persian Gulf, except Iraq, reached agreement with the companies on 25% participation, which was to enter into force as of January 1, 1973. The question arises why did the producers hesitate to nationalize the industry, especially after Algeria successfully nationalized 51% of the French oil companies operating in her territory, and after Iraq nationalized the Iraq Petroleum Company?

All the producing countries knew that they were not ready to operate the industry themselves, and were dependent on the concessionaire companies. But they did not know how far they could press the companies. They were afraid that if they pressed them too hard and too fast the companies might surrender their concessions, and the operation of the industry would fall on them.

Saudi Arabia, which was the largest producer in the Middle East, was also the weakest in terms of economic development and in ability to operate the industry. She, therefore, watched very carefully the development of relations between the producers and the companies.

The companies had two considerations: their obligation to supply oil to their customers, private and governmental, and profits. They all understood that the profits would decrease as the producers' participation share would increase. But the obligation to the customers was an important consideration to the companies and the consuming countries. The greater the successes of OPEC the greater became the temptation to press the companies more and more. At some point of diminishing profits the companies would give up their undertakings. The producers, however, did not know where that point was.

Saudi Arabia was, therefore, satisfied with 20% participation, which was subsequently raised to 25% with a proviso for gradual increases until it would reach 51% in 1982, as mentioned above. Saudi Arabia believed that by that date she would have advanced in the administrative and other aspects of the industry and would know at what point the company would refuse to cooperate with the government.

Iran, on her part, watched closely the development of relations between the companies and the Arab producers of the Persian Gulf, in order to formulate her own oil policy. Theoretically, Iran did not face a participation issue, for she had nationalized her industry in 1951.

After the impressive achievements of OPEC, Iran was willing to attempt full control of her oil industry not only theoretically, but also practically, without completely destroying the Consortium, which remained the major source of her income, and for the international market of her oil. The Shah tried to take over control of the production and refining facilities and convert the Consortium into a mere sales agency, for which services it would receive either a sales commission or a discount from the current oil price. Yet he was anxious to retain the services of the Consortium, and the participation of the Consortium companies in the further development of the industry on the basis of joint-ventures. Iran faced the same question as the other producers: how far would the Consortium be willing to submit to Iran's demands, and at what point would it surrender its concession?

In the meanwhile the Kuwait National Assembly rejected the government agreement with the company for 25% participation; some members of the Assembly demanded 60% participation, while others demanded full nationalization. The Kuwait government entered new negotiations with the Kuwait Oil Company for 60% participation. Saudi Arabia followed suit.

In spite of the general agitation in the Arab world, or perhaps because of it, for nationalization of the oil industry, the Saudi Arabian Oil Minister, Yamani, stated at the end of April 1973, that since the industrial world depended on oil, Saudi Arabia was ready to do everything in her power to guarantee the flow of the oil to its destinations. He stated that the producers must not nationalize their oil, for they were not qualified to wrestle with the two most crucial aspects of the industry: exploration and marketing.

While in London in the middle of June 1972, the Shah announced a new program which was to solve the oil problem in his country: maximum output, maximum security of supply, stability of conditions for the period of the agreement, and after that, far-reaching changes in the terms of operations. This program aimed, on the one hand, to increase oil production, and as a result, the revenue which

Iran needed for her very ambitious long-range economic development program, and on the other hand, to make the transition from the Consortium to the National Iranian Oil Company as easy as possible without major shocks and under optimal conditions. To test the workability of the program, Iran demanded that the Consortium increase daily production at a rate that would have it reaching 8 million barrels at the end of the 'seventies. At the same time the Iranian government announced that NIOC would assume greater and direct responsibility in all branches of the industry, from exploitation through marketing, and that NIOC would take over the Abadan refinery.

The Consortium companies refused, at first, to accept Iran's terms. The Shah thereupon announced that if the companies refused to comply with the terms offered them the government would take over the entire industry and would not renew the agreement with the Consortium after 1979. However, should they agree to accept the proferred terms, Iran would be willing to continue to supply the oil at special prices for a certain period of time beyond 1979.

The member companies of the Consortium had a choice: either refuse the government proposals and insist on the terms of the original agreement, but with a certainty that they would obtain no oil after the expiry of the agreement in 1979, or accept the new terms and assure themselves oil supplies a number of years beyond 1979.

While they were pondering the choice, the Shah took the risk and announced on March 20, 1973, that the Iranian government had taken over the control of the operation of the oil industry, and that he had forced the Consortium to transfer operations to NIOC. He also reported that Iran planned to invest $1 billion in order to double production in 1978.

The Consortium surrendered. On March 21 it signed a new agreement the terms of which were dictated by Iran. They provided that the Consortium would continue to operate all the different aspects of the industry. However, the Consortium became primarily a sales agent for the oil produced, and obligated itself to purchase, under a vague formula, 4,866,000 barrels of oil a day and become a partner, up to 40% in new and huge projects for the development of the oil resources of the country. Those projects were to be under the total control of the National Iranian Oil Company.[1]

(1) These provisions of the agreement caused, early in 1976, a crisis in the relations between Iran and the member-companies of the Consortium. The general reduction in oil consumption which followed the steep price increases in 1973 and 1974, and the high price set for Iranian oil forced the Consortium companies to reduce their crude oil purchases. NIOC charged that the companies lifted an average of 4,236,000 barrels a day during 1975, and in the last quarter of the year the average dropped to 3,687,000 barrels. NIOC also claimed that the companies failed to invest some $150 million for

The developments in Iran influenced and were influenced by the developments in the other parts of the region. Saudi Arabia realized that the companies were ready to continue with the exploitation of the oil even if the producing countries were in full control of the operation of the industry. She was, therefore, determined to demand 60% participation right away and not wait until 1982 for 51%.

In the middle of June 1973, as mentioned above, Kuwait asked for 60% participation. (In the meantime she cut production, for conservation purposes, to 3 million barrels a day). Both Kuwait and Saudi Arabia challenged the validity of the Teheran 1971 agreement. On September 7, the Saudi Arabian Oil Minister, Yamani, declared that the Teheran agreement which was to regulate oil prices until 1975 was dead, and it must be replaced by a new agreement which will serve the producers' interests. He asked for new negotiations between producers and the companies which would establish a new basis for posted prices and which would increase the producers' revenue. He warned "if we fail to obtain the cooperation of the oil companies in amending the Teheran price agreement, we would have to exercise our rights on our own."[2]

As 25% participation was the general formula for practically the entire Middle East, except Iran and Bahrain, in 1973, so 60% became the general formula in 1974. In spite of the extremists' demands for full nationalization, the Kuwait National Assembly approved in May 1974 the 60% participation agreement. It was to be in effect as of January 1, 1974. Compensation was set at $112 million. The terms were to be reevaluated at the end of 1979. An Aramco spokesman in New York announced early in July 1974, that as of January 1, Saudi Arabia's share in the company would be 60% instead of 25%: But the Saudi Arabian government declared that in addition to the increased participation share it would demand a new basis for its relations with

the second half of 1975, and about $30 million for the first month of 1976. The drop in sales of crude created a deficit of $2.4 billion in the Iranian budget. In February 1976, the Prime Minister, Amir Abbas Hoveida blamed the companies for a $3 billion fall in revenue. Both the Shah and the Prime Minister issued threatening warnings to the companies.

The companies called for modifications in the 1973 agreement, both in the magnitude of the purchases and in the extent of the investments, in view of the changed conditions. At first Iran maintained that she would not cut prices in order to increase oil sales, and insisted on full compliance with the terms of the 1973 agreement, and broke off negotiations with the companies under the threat of cancelling the agreement. However, early in March NIOC announced a cut of 9.5 cents per barrel in the price. It also resumed, late in April, negotiations with the companies. Whether the 9.5 cents price-cut will increase the oil sales and restore Iran's oil revenue, only time will tell.

(2) The October 1973 Arab-Israel war broke out in the meantime, which resulted in the Arab oil embargo, the huge price increases, and the subsequent lifting of the embargo. These will be dealt with in following chapters. These developments inevitably affected basically the issues of participation and nationalization.

the American company. Reliable sources in Beirut reported that at the meetings in New York between company representatives and the Saudi Arabian Oil Minister, the latter demanded full nationalization, and that the buy-back price for the company was to be the full international market price without any discount; for operation, administration and technological services the company would be paid stated fees.

According to other sources, Yamani proposed that in return for its services after nationalization, the company was to purchase the entire oil output at a 7% discount from the current international price. At the end Saudi Arabia agreed to 60% participation. But Yamani predicted that by the end of 1974 his country would have nationalized the oil industry with Aramco's consent.

After Kuwait and Saudi Arabia raised their participation share to 60%, Abu Dhabi followed suit on the same terms, so did Oman. Bahrain, which originally was not interested in participation, now demanded and obtained from the Bahrain Oil Company, a retroactive 25% participation for the year 1973 and 60% from January 1, 1974. Qatar also raised its share from 25% to 60% participation.

Since the companies agreed to continue to operate even after the producers obtained 60% participation and gained full control of the companies, it was inevitable that the next demand would be 100% takeover. Early in 1975 it was reported that Aramco agreed, in principle, to complete nationalization and to transfer all the company properties to the government.

But in spite of the constant threats from the producers on the one side and the readiness of the companies to recognize, at least in principle, nationalization on the other, there was some hesitation in the producing countries to take the last step. The march in this direction was begun by a rather minor producer. Early in 1975 the government of Dubai announced that it had acquired all the oil and natural gas facilities in its territory. Dubai was thus the first producer in the Persian Gulf area to gain full control of its oil industry. The Shaikh announced that the companies would receive $110 million as compensation for their shares in the companies.

In the middle of March 1975, the Government of Bahrain stated that it intended to assume 100% ownership of its oil industry. It said that the "participation agreement of November 23, 1974 will be considered as an interim agreement until a new agreement is concluded. The Ministry of Finance and National Economy will lay down the principles on which this agreement will be based."

On December 22, 1974, Qatar announced that it would shortly begin talks with the foreign oil companies operating in her territory for the acquisition of their 40% equity of their holdings. At the end of April

1975, the oil minister said that within the next ten days his government would take over the remaining 40% of the companies' equity, for which they would be paid $35 million. Yet, early in January 1976, the Qatar Government reported that negotiations on details were proceeding.

The Kuwait Government decided in March 1975 to take over the last 40% equity of the two foreign companies, British Petroleum and Gulf Oil. Negotiations with the companies proceeded, and early in December agreement was reached. The companies were to receive $50.5 million compensation; they were to be entitled to purchase 950,000 barrels a day during the next five years with an option to buy no less than 400,000 barrels a day for five further years. They were to be entitled to a 15-cent discount per barrel off the government official selling price of crude oil.

While negotiating for the transfer, the Kuwait Oil Minister declared in September 1975 that his government did not want BP and Gulf to leave the country after nationalization. Rather, the Government wished to join the two companies in joint ventures in Kuwait and elsewhere, and wanted the companies to provide the Kuwait National Agency with their technology.[3]

The relations between the Iraq government and the Iraq Petroleum Company had been tense ever since Abd al-Karim Qassem enacted the December 1961 oil law, which limited the Company to the areas actually worked at the time. This meant the confiscation of over 99% of the original concession territories, including North Rumaila field which was drilled but not yet worked by the Basrah Petroleum

(3) Marketing was one of the most difficult aspects of total takeover, for it was controlled by the companies. Kuwait attempted to solve it by direct long term sales to foreign companies. Thus early in January 1975, Kuwait concluded an agreement with Maruzen Oil for the purchase of 10,000 barrels a day, at 93% of posted price. In the middle of the month she signed a contract with the Royal Dutch-Shell Company for delivery of 400,000 barrels daily. It was for a three-year period at 93% of posted price subject to change in line with OPEC decisions. Early in March, Exxon signed a three-year contract for the purchase of 50,000 barrels a day as of March 1, to rise to 100,000 barrels as of July 1, terms as those with Royal Dutch-Shell. On April 10, Idemitsu signed a three-year agreement for the purchase of 50,000 barrels daily. Terms the same as those with Exxon. Thus in the first four months of 1975, Kuwait succeeded in contracting direct sales of 560,000 barrels daily with companies which had no equity in Kuwait concessions.

Early in September 1975, the Kuwaiti Minister of Oil said that by October the direct sales quantity was scheduled to rise to 815,000 barrels a day. Yet because of the very narrow margin granted Gulf and BP in the price of oil, they failed to sell the agreed upon quantities, after the full takeover of the Kuwait Oil Company. Despite the increase in world demand for oil in the latter part of 1976, Kuwait announced early in January 1977 that she would cut oil production because her customers have decided to reduce their purchases. Nevertheless, Kuwait voted at the OPEC Conference in Doha in the middle of December 1976 for a 10% price increase, and criticized Saudi Arabia for increasing the price by only 5%.

Company.   After Abd al-Rahman Arif came to power the Company hoped for an improvement in relations and even for a modification of the December 1961 law.   However, after the July 1968 revolution, which brought to power Ahmad Hasan Bakr, relations between the government and the oil company rapidly deteriorated.

As was mentioned above (Chapter III) Iraq benefited from the closure of the Suez Canal and she obtained special premiums for her oil which flowed to the Mediterranean ports.   As a result Iraq was interested in increasing the output of the northern oil fields.   In line with the OPEC recommendations Iraq demanded 20% participation in the company.   At the same time she demanded a general 10% increase in production, but a 17% increase in the oil exported from the Mediterranean ports.   The company, on its part, requested that Iraq agree to go to arbitration on the question of the confiscation of the concession areas, especially that of North Rumaila.   The Iraq Government countered with a demand of 95.6 million Iraqi Dinars for retroactive royalty payments.

On May 17, 1972 the government delivered an ultimatum to the company: either it comply within two weeks with the government request or special legislation would be enacted against the company, obviously meaning nationalization.   The chairman of the company's Board of Directors came to Baghdad with counterproposals.   They were rejected.

The developments to June 1972 clearly demonstrated cause and effect.   Since the per barrel revenue to the Iraq Government from the northern fields was higher than that from the southern fields, it urged the company to increase production from the northern fields. But the demand for oil in Europe was lower than expected and the price of tanker transportation dropped.   It was, therefore, more economical to ship oil from the southern fields than pay the extra premium for the oil from the northern fields.   The company therefore, increased production in the southern fields and decreased production from the northern fields.   Government revenue fell during the later part of 1971 and the early part of 1972.   The company maintained that economic considerations determined its production policy, while the government charged that it was a pressure tactic to force the return of the North Rumaila field.

On June 1, 1972, the President of Iraq announced, in a nationwide radio and television broadcast, the nationalization of the Iraq Petroleum Company.   Neither the Mosul nor the Basrah companies were included.[4]

(4) The organizational structure of the Iraq Petroleum Company is a bit complicated. The concession in the northwestern part of the country was granted to the Iraq Petroleum

On June 9, OPEC at an extraordinary conference resolved to support Iraq's action, and requested all members not to permit oil production increases in their territories to make up the deficit of Iraq oil.[5] Also, OAPEC met in Baghdad and expressed support of Iraq's and Syria's action.

After prolonged negotiations with the company, the President of Iraq announced on February 28, 1973, that a final settlement with the company was reached. The company was to pay the government £ 141 million in settlement of all claims. The government was to give the company 15 million tons of crude oil from the Kirkuk fields free of charge as compensation for nationalizing the industry. The Mosul Petroleum Company surrendered its concession to the government.

The operation of the oil industry and especially putting the North Rumaila field in operation presented formidable difficulties. After some hesitation, Iraq—with the direct financial and technical assistance from the Soviet Union and the other Communist countries —succeeded in both. However, the most challenging aspect of nationalization was finding markets for the oil produced, even though in much reduced quantities. It is very likely that the "high-risk gamble" as the *New York Times* described it, would have ended in ignominious disaster, had it not been for the 1973 oil embargo which opened up unexpectedly new and great markets for Iraqi oil.

Not to risk all, Iraq did not nationalize the Basrah Petroleum Company in June 1972 although it was an integral part of the Iraq Petroleum Company. In the above February 1973 agreement the Basrah Petroleum Company obligated itself to increase production from 32 million tons in 1972 to 35 million in 1973, to 45 million in 1974, to 65 million in 1975 and to 80 million tons in 1976. Through this agreement the Iraq Government guaranteed for itself not only the disposition of the oil from the southern fields in ever increasing quantities, but also a goodly share of its oil revenue.

Even after the outbreak of the October 1973 war, Iraq did not nationalize the entire Basrah Petroleum Company. On October 7,

Company, the concession in the northeastern part was granted to the Mosul Petroleum Company, and the concession in the southern part was granted to the Basrah Petroleum Company. But the last two were in fact subsidiaries of the Iraq Petroleum Company. The latter was owned 23.75% each by British Petroleum, Royal Dutch-Shell, Compagnie Francaise des Petroles and the Near East Development Company (Exxon and Mobil), and 5% by Partex (Gulbenkian Foundation).

(5) According to the *New York Times* of January 14, 1973, the nationalization caused a sharp decline in exports and disrupted Iraq's development plan as well as transit income for oil shipments through Syria and Lebanon. Nevertheless, Saudi Arabia, Iran and the Persian Gulf Amirates stepped up production and increased their revenue.

the government reported that it had nationalized the shares of the American companies (Exxon and Mobil) because of the United States' support of Israel. On October 21, the government nationalized the Royal Dutch-Shell share for Holland's support of Israel. On December 20, the government also nationalized the Partex share because the Partex Foundation was registered in Portugal, and that country permitted the extension of United States help to Israel from her territory. When participation was extended to 60%, Iraq obtained 60% participation in the company. In the middle of December 1975, President Bakr announced in Baghdad the complete takeover of the remaining foreign holdings of the Basrah Petroleum Company.

After long negotiations it was reported in Washington, in the latter part of March 1976, that Aramco agreed to total takeover by the Saudi Arabian Government. The terms included, in addition to compensation, a service payment of 20 to 22 cents for each barrel lifted by the Aramco companies, this would amount to payments by Saudi Arabia to the companies of about $1.6 million a day, at the current production rate.

Only Abu Dhabi was not ready for total nationalization of the oil industry. Her Oil Minister stated at the end of April 1975, that his country was not capable of operating the oil industry by her own efforts, and rejected, therefore, plans for a total takeover. It is very likely that the foreign companies in Abu Dhabi reached the point where they were no longer ready to cooperate with the government, in spite of the fact that they still retained 40% equity in the concessions. Their profits were so low that they refused to invest any additional funds in the development of the energy resources of Abu Dhabi.

Indeed, at the end of November of that year the Abu Dhabi Government announced that it had decided that the Abu Dhabi National Oil Company would erect by itself a huge, $1.2 billion natural gas liquefaction plant, because the foreign oil companies refused to contribute their share in the joint-venture.

It would seem that the pattern of relationship between producer and company set by Iran and now followed by Dubai, Kuwait, Saudi Arabia and Iraq would become the general practice throughout the Middle East; and the role of the concessionaire companies would have been radically changed.

7 The Arab Oil Embargo

On October 16, 1973 right after the outbreak of hostilities between the Arabs and Israel, the oil ministers of the Arab countries gathered in Kuwait to discuss the consequences of the war. On the following day they unanimously decided to cut oil supplies to the consuming countries at the rate of 5% per month, and to impose a total embargo on the United States and Holland, because of their support of Israel. The embargo and the cut in supplies were to continue until Israel would withdraw from all the Arab areas she occupied, including Jerusalem, and the rights of the Palestinians were guaranteed. It was also decided to increase unilaterally, by 70%, the posted prices of oil.

Some Arab producers jumped the gun and cut supplies by more than 5% per month. When, therefore, OAPEC reconvened in Kuwait on November 5, it decided to limit the total cut to no more than 25% from the October 1, 1973 level.

A careful analysis of the various decisions of OAPEC conferences reveals that there was no coherent and systematic planning either in the terms of the embargo or in the conditions for its lifting. For in spite of the November 5 decision, Ahmad Zaki al-Yamani, the Saudi Arabian oil minister, who travelled all over the United States and Europe in an effort to pressure the consuming countries to side with the Arabs against Israel, threatened on November 23 in Copenhagen —where the Foreign Ministers of the European Common Market met secretly to discuss the energy crisis—that the cut of oil supplies might reach, should it become necessary, as high as 80%.

For the purpose of the embargo OAPEC classified the consuming countries as "friendly", "neutral" and "hostile" depending on their position in the Arab-Israeli conflict. Britain, France and Spain were classified as "friendly" and the embargo was not to have applied to them. However, when OAPEC met in Vienna on November 18 it decided that the 5% cut in supplies for December would not be applied to all the countries of the European Common Market in consideration of their recognition of the Arab demands (the Brussels

November 6 Declaration). However, the December 9 meeting, which took place in Kuwait, decided that the January cut in supplies would apply to all countries, hostile as well as friendly.

At the same time a substantial retreat occurred in the conditions for lifting the embargo. From the full Israeli withdrawal, the demands were reduced to a time-table of Israeli withdrawals guaranteed by the United States. However, the OAPEC conference of December 25 decided, instead of cutting supplies, to increase them by 10% during the month of January 1974, and to gather in Tripoli, Libya on February 13 to deal with the embargo question. In the meantime, on December 23, the oil ministers of the Persian Gulf countries, members of OPEC, met and decided to raise the posted price of crude oil to $11.65 a barrel, an increase of more than 400% from the $2.59 price on October 1, 1973.

From the OAPEC meeting of December 25, 1973 to the Vienna meeting which ended on March 18, 1974, Saudi Arabia and Egypt made a continuous and relentless effort, which was finally crowned with success, to lift the embargo. It could safely be assumed that in his peripatetic travels in the Middle East, at the end of 1973, Dr. Henry Kissinger, United States Secretary of State, received a definite promise, among many others, that the oil embargo would be lifted, and that an official announcement to that effect would be made at the OAPEC Tripoli meeting scheduled for February 13. This was intentionally or unintentionally leaked to the press. However, instead of waiting for that date, President Richard Nixon—for his own reasons—declared in his State of the Union address to Congress on January 1, 1974 that reliable Arab leadership sources assured him that the oil embargo would be lifted even before the convening of the OAPEC meeting in the middle of February. This announcement of the President caused a furor in the Arab world, and OAPEC found itself in a serious crisis. Iraq, which did not participate in the embargo and opposed all its aspects (she maintained that the only solution to the oil problem and the elimination of the concessionaire companies was nationalization of the foreign companies) boycotted the Tripoli meeting. Saudi Arabia and Egypt strongly advocated the lifting of the embargo, while the radical countries—Syria (a minor exporter to Western consuming countries), Algeria and Libya (which did not comply with the embargo)—opposed the lifting of the embargo. As the time of the Tripoli meeting was approaching it became clear that the sharp differences of opinion between the advocates and the opponents of lifting the embargo might cause the breakup of OAPEC. Moreover, the United States, for whom the advocates asked the lifting of the embargo, openly challenged and defied the oil producing countries by calling a conference of all the great consuming countries in Washington for early in February to work out plans against the dangers of the embargo and against OPEC. (See Chapter VIII below)

In order to prevent a breakup of OAPEC, a small Arab summit conference was called for February 12, in Algiers. The participants were the King of Saudi Arabia and the presidents of Egypt, Syria and Algeria; the agenda consisted of two items: the lifting of the oil embargo against the United States and the terms for the separation of forces between Syria and Israel. The differences between the advocates and the opponents of the lifting of the embargo persisted, but all participants agreed that the Tripoli meeting must be postponed. It was also decided to send a delegation of the foreign ministers of Saudi Arabia and Egypt (the two countries which advocated the lifting of the embargo) to Washington to persuade the United States to accept the Syrian terms for the separation of forces and impose them on Israel. This would soften the opposition to lifting the embargo. The effort was fruitless, and the delegation returned home without convincing the United States of the desirability of meeting Syria's demands.

Egypt was determined, as was Saudi Arabia, to lift the embargo as quickly as possible, and on March 3, she asked for the convening of the Tripoli meeting. Five of the big oil producers were for lifting the embargo. (On that day the separation of forces agreement between Israel and Egypt was completed). The general opinion was that the lifting of the embargo depended on the separation of forces between Israel and Syria. But Egypt was not willing to wait any longer, and decided to convene the conference even in face of strong opposition by the radical countries. On March 7, Rahman al-Atiqi, Kuwaiti Finance and Oil Minister, announced that the conference was scheduled to meet on March 10 in Cairo. Libya and Algeria, however, quickly denied both the time and the place of the conference. On March 11, after a number of oil ministers have arrived in Cairo it was decided to hold the conference in Tripoli on March 13.

The sessions of the conference were closed and stormy, but it became known nevertheless that a majority of the participants was for lifting the embargo. Libya, however, refused to permit the announcement to that effect to come from her soil. It was, therefore, decided to announce the decision after a meeting in Vienna where the ministers were gathering for an OPEC conference. An effort would be made in Vienna to arrive at a unanimous decision. After a three-day debate, the effort failed and the conference decided by a vote of 7 producers to lift the embargo; Algeria stated that she would lift the embargo temporarily, and Syria and Libya said they would continue with it. The decision made no mention about restoring the supply cuts, but the Saudi Arabian oil minister made it clear that supplies would be reinstated to the October 1, 1973 level. In spite of the decision that OAPEC was to reconsider the question at its June meeting in Cairo, and should the United States policy not be satisfactory the embargo could be reimposed, it was clearly understood by all, both advocates and opponents of the decision, that the embargo would not be renewed.

The proclamation of the embargo and original extreme demands for its lifting and its cancellation after less than five months, without the fulfillment of the stated conditions, except the separation of forces agreement between Egypt and Israel, are puzzling and need elucidation.

The motives of the Egyptians were obvious.   Dr. Kissinger succeeded, through his tactics, to save Egypt from total military defeat, he believed that he extricated Egypt from the iron grip of the Soviet Union and he succeeded in bringing about the separation of forces between Egypt and Israel.   Egypt was ready to exploit the United States and demand the fulfillment of the commitments which Kissinger no doubt had made to her, thus challenging the Soviet Union. But it would be impossible to demand anything from the United States while an Arab oil embargo was still in force against her.

Saudi Arabia's motives for the lifting of the embargo were more complex.   Throughout the entire period of oil production in the Middle East two struggles were carried on.   One was between the producing countries and the concessionaire companies.   In this struggle the companies held the upper hand until the late 'sixties.   Since then and especially since 1970 the situation was completely reversed.   In a very short time and at a rapid pace the producers succeeded in gaining control over the oil industry and they gained the upper hand over the companies.   This reversal of roles could be explained by the political international position of the producing countries and by the conditions which prevailed during the different periods of the growth of the oil industry.

Since the outbreak of World War II, the producers realized the great importance and value of the oil in their territories.   They appreciated that the oil was an exhaustible resource and was constantly being diminished.   They therefore were determined to exploit it wisely and under conditions which would benefit them most.   They fought with the companies to obtain a greater share of the profits from the oil produced, and better conditions for its exploitation.   The companies, however, refused consistently, persistently and successfully to respond to the demands of the producers, because they held all the good "cards" in the game of the oil industry. They possessed all the means necessary to operate and develop the industry, and they were in complete and total control of it. They had the technological know-how and the financial resources necessary to operate and manage this very complex industry; they had all the world oil markets and they were in a position to control production in order to enlarge their profits.

In comparison with the companies, the producers were powerless; they depended, almost exclusively, on the oil companies for their regular budgets and for other governmental expenses. Should they threaten the companies with a stoppage of the flow of oil from their territories, the companies could command replacements from other oil regions, especially from the United States. The greatest weapon in the hands of the companies was the fact that throughout the entire period of oil production in the Middle East—except during wars and political crises—there was an over-supply of oil in world markets. The demand for oil was much smaller than the supply. Under such circumstances the producers could not obtain any concessions from the companies.

At the end of the 'sixties and at the beginning of the 'seventies conditions began to change; the demand for oil and oil products rose constantly and soon surpassed the supply. The thirst of the industrialized and developing countries for ever greater quantities of oil could not be slaked. At the same time the oil reserves and oil production in the United States began to decline.

On the other hand, some of the producing countries began to penetrate, even then—on a limited scale at first—the technology of the industry and started to produce, refine, transport and even market some of the oil. But what was perhaps most decisive—because of enormous production quantities—they earned fantastically huge amounts of revenue, and were no longer in need of additional income, indeed some of them had more money than they knew what to do with. To this should be added the impact of the world inflationary pressures and the instability of the international financial and currency structures which gave the producing countries great financial and political influence and power.

The Middle East oil crisis which stemmed from purely economic factors suddenly assumed aspects of political determinants. The most outstanding Arab oil-producing countries' spokesmen, ignoring the global superpower struggle and all the international economic and financial aspects of the crisis, proclaimed in various parts of the world that the energy crisis was a purely political issue; they reduced it to simplistic terms. The world energy shortage was caused by Israel.

All the world had to do was force Israel to comply with Arab demands and it would get all the oil it wanted at former prices. The supposed threatened disaster which faced Europe, Japan and even the United States could easily and simply be avoided and the prosperity and well-being of all could continue and blossom if only Israel would do the bidding of the Arabs.

Motives for the Embargo

The second struggle was among the Arab countries themselves for involving the oil in the strife of their national movement. The history of the Arab national unity struggle did not commence in October 1973. Ever since the Arab League professionals realized the importance of oil to the world they attempted to exploit it for the political cause, but they failed in their effort until October 1973. The major oil producers, Saudi Arabia and Iraq at first, and Kuwait and Libya later, consistently refused to permit their oil to become a football in the hands of the Arab League politicians; they would not allow the non-oil-producing members of the League to use their oil freely and irresponsibly. The producers looked upon their oil during the entire period as a strictly national economic resource which each country must protect and control without involving it in the risks of the complicated Arab political battle. It was already mentioned above that the original purpose of the formation of OAPEC was to prevent other Arab countries, especially Egypt, from interfering with the economic interests of the producers.

The question then arises, why did the great Arab oil-producers suddenly change their position and agreed to proclaim the embargo, and thus involve their oil in the Arab political strife? Why was Saudi Arabia the leader in the embargo tactic? The answer to these questions lies in the changed conditions of the producing countries. It is submitted that the underlying determinants in the energy crisis were and remained economic, that the Middle East oil producers were aligned for the purpose of obtaining the highest price for their product and gaining control of the industry. The world energy crisis made this possible as the Middle East oil became indispensable in the economic and industrial life of the Western countries. For the first time in the history of the Arab national movement both the political and economic aims coincided. The Arab leadership under King Faisal exploited the situation and assumed a political stance in proclaiming the oil embargo. It was utilized to reinforce the real economic factors and to rally, to the side of the producers, the loyalty and following of the Arab masses. Paradoxically, King Faisal, the arch conservative and pro-Western oriented Arab leader, had become the radical front runner in the battle against the Western countries, and especially against the United States.

Why then was Saudi Arabia so anxious and determined to lift the embargo? The fateful decision of March 18, 1974 to lift the Arab oil embargo brought to an end the first and grand attempt of the Arab producing countries to employ their oil in the political struggle against the Western countries. A careful analysis of the outcome of the attempt would reveal that it was a failure, except for one thing —the real objective: tremendously large increases in the posted prices. The size of the increases frightened Saudi Arabia, the leader of the embargo movement; for she believed that in the end the increases might defeat the purpose of the effort.

The reasons for the failure stem from the very structure of the group of the Middle East producing countries, from the deep differences among them and from the various motives in proclaiming the embargo.

The oil producing countries are divided into three categories, and these categories determined their position on the embargo. The first group consists of countries or Amirates of the Persian Gulf which depend heavily or exclusively on their oil income. They are either just on the threshold of oil development (Dubai) or are old small and limited producers (Bahrain). They would be ready to sell their oil according to their original contracts and concessions without imposing special conditions. The second group consists of countries which have large populations, massive development projects, and are great oil producers. In this category are included Iran, Iraq and Algeria. They need the oil revenue to finance their current budgets and their economic programs. They would be ready to sell all the oil the consumers could purchase provided the price was high, and if possible very high. The third group consists of countries with small populations, gigantic oil resources and production records, and financial saturation. To this category belong Saudi Arabia, Kuwait and Abu Dhabi. They would be ready to curtail production to the industrialized nations in order to achieve their economic and financial objectives.

But the Arab oil-producing countries are also divided into two other categories: the conservative and the radical nations, each group of which had opposing objectives in the promulgation of the embargo. The conservative group had primarily economic aims, and when these were fulfilled they were ready to lift the embargo, without any further disturbance to the international relations structure of the region. The radical countries on the other hand had political-ideological aims, and they saw in the embargo a means of changing the political-ideological-social pattern of the Arab world; an excellent opportunity to gain control of the Arab movement and utilize the embargo for the Arab social revolution. These deep differences were, in fact, the cause for the struggle before and at the Tripoli conference, and later at the Vienna meeting.

There could be no doubt that Saudi Arabia emerged the victor in this battle. For her the embargo was a means to attain a reasonable increase in the oil revenue. King Faisal never sought the objectives of the Arab socialist countries, and certainly not those of the Soviet Union. When, therefore, his objective was achieved by the very high increases in the posted prices, he hastened to resume the shipping of oil to the Western world. He communicated this determination to the United States through his spokesmen.

The radical countries Iraq, Syria, Algeria and Libya were alarmed at Faisal's determination and opposed any attempts to lift the embargo. The Soviet Union, naturally, supported the radical countries and advocated the continuation of the embargo; it accused Saudi Arabia of betraying the cause of Arab nationalism.

Another factor which made Saudi Arabia eager to lift the embargo was her nature and position as a small oil producer in the Middle East, in contrast to the second greatest producer in the area: Iran. It should be noted that the issue of alternatives for Middle East oil is not one of research and discovery. The alternatives, and they are many in number, are available, the question is merely one of effectuating them. They were not put in operation until now for two reasons which are the two sides of the same coin: the relatively cheap cost of Middle East oil and the very high cost of the various possible alternatives. Iran, which has grandiose economic development projects which run into many billions of dollars, is not interested in conserving her oil resources. On the contrary, she is determined to exploit them in very huge quantities and in the shortest period of time as long as the price is very high. She should be ready to exploit her oil within the next ten years. During this period she would receive sufficient funds —should the prices be high—to enable her to develop new economic resources which would make her independent of oil income. During the next ten years no alternatives could be activated that would compete with her oil. The oil that would remain after that period she could use for her own industrial needs, and would not be interested in selling it in competition with the alternatives. Iran was, therefore, throughout the entire period, the consistent and persistent advocate of oil price increases.

Saudi Arabia, in contrast, is not economically developed, and her development programs are not realizable immediately, or even in the foreseeable future.[1]

Saudi Arabia expects that oil will be the major, if not exclusive, source of revenue during the next fifty years or even one hundred years. She could not, therefore, risk her future by limiting supplies and by increasing prices too high. Those actions would hasten the activation of the oil alternatives. Hence her anxiety and determination to lift the embargo, and her readiness to reduce the posted prices in order to slow down or even stop completely the efforts to activate alternatives, especially in the United States. Similar considerations prompted Kuwait and Abu Dhabi to demand the lifting of the embargo.[2]

The embargo and the subsequent development—even after it was lifted—strengthened the position of OPEC. It was OPEC which decided on the very high price increases at the end of December 1973, and the additional increase in September 1975. In spite of Saudi Arabia's efforts—weak to be sure—to reduce or at least to freeze prices, they remained stable from December 1973 to September 1975 and then rose by another 10% (See above chapter 1). The producers succeeded in increasing their oil revenue, in addition to the price increases, by acquiring 60% participation in the companies, and by raises in the royalty rates and in the governments' share in the profits of the companies' 40% equity in the concessions. As was indicated in the previous chapter, the drive was for full nationalization.

The huge success of OPEC on one hand, and the hesitations of Saudi Arabia about pressing too hard for reduced prices on the other were the direct results of the weakness and lack of unity and determination of the consuming countries and their almost eager readiness to respond not only to the pressure of the Arab oil producing countries through political threats, but also to pay the high prices. At first Saudi Arabia and even Iran were frightened by the willingness, nay eagerness, of the consuming nations to pay, in open tender, as high as $17-27 for a barrel of oil.

---

(1) In September 1974 the Saudi Arabian Government approved a new five-year development program to start January 1975, and allotted it $60 billion, six times the budgeted sum for the previous five-year plan which ended in 1974. Hisham Nazir, Minister of State and President of the Central Planning Organization stated, in making the announcement: "We had given ourselves 30-40 years to create, through sustained development, a new income base which can replace revenues derived from oil, and we hope to meet the target". He admitted, however, that the long term goal of lessening dependence on oil revenues would be difficult to fulfill in the next 20-25 years, during which, in fact this dependence would steadily rise as the need for capital funding would continue to grow.
(2) During a visit in the middle of October 1975 in Bonn, the Saudi Arabian oil minister stated that his country was advocating a reduction in posted prices below a level that would make other energy supplies competitive in price.

The question of the buy-back prices which the companies were to pay for the governments' participation oil slowed down, to some extent the process of complete control and domination of the industry by the producers. They faced a number of problems resulting from their participation achievement. Would the companies be ready to commit themselves to buy back the participation oil? What should be the extent of the commitment on their side to sell back the oil to the companies? Should this commitment be for a long period? For if the producers could find markets for their oil they would not be able to supply their potential purchasers. What should be the price level, in relation to the posted prices, at which the companies would be willing to buy back the oil?

Saudi Arabia evolved a complicated formula which guaranteed a reasonable supply to the companies and sufficient oil for the markets which she could find in the earlier years, and a smaller supply to the companies and a larger quantity for herself to market directly in later years.

After the embargo the producers tried to raise the buy back prices to 96% of the posted prices. The companies refused to pay such high prices; the producers, therefore, attempted to offer the oil in open tender. But there were no bidders. Kuwait forced the two parent companies of the Kuwait Oil Company to pay the high prices she demanded under a threat of a drastic cut in production. Other smaller producers were forced to reduce the buy back prices to almost 80% of the postal prices.

It would seem that one of the deterrents against full nationalization was the buy back prices. Since the oil markets were still in the hands of the companies and the open tenders did not produce the desired results, it was preferable that the companies retain at least 40% of the concessions so that they would be interested in their equity oil and would be more amenable to buy back the participation at rather high prices. This was the dilemma of the producers. Should they nationalize the industry completely or let the companies retain 40%? Since the producers did not dare to recklessly increase the posted prices, OPEC decided in December 1973 that the economic committee of the organization, which is composed of the oil specialists of the members, should meet every three months and recommend price levels. The committee met duly every three months, and recommended—out of economic considerations—increases in the posted price. But each time the plenary decided—for its own reasons—against the increases. OPEC nevertheless decided, as mentioned above, on raises in the royalty rates, and in the governments' share in the profits. The major argument for the raises was that the companies' profits were too high and they must be reduced. However, these raises might increase the cost of the equity oil for the companies as much as the participation oil. If the companies refused to pay the high prices for participation oil, they surely would reject the concession oil if it cost as high as participation oil.

The risk and the calculations were obvious. Would the pressure of the consuming countries on the companies for their oil supplies be strong enough as to force them to agree to the high royalties and a high government profit share, which would equal participation prices, or would the companies surrender their concessions totally and refuse to buy oil except in free competition among the producers. The producers believed that through pressure and contracts, the companies would pay the posted prices. They, therefore, proceeded with full nationalization of the oil industry.[3]

In spite of the warnings of neutral, non-interested oil specialists about the coming energy crisis, in spite of the high rise in the demand for petroleum throughout the world, and the parallel decline, both in oil reserves and production in the United States, the Administration in Washington did nothing to prevent or at least ease the oncoming energy crisis. The big oil companies which exerted great influence in Washington succeeded in lulling the American public into a sense of false security as to a coming oil crisis. They attempted to convince the public and the government that the crisis was not economic but political; that affairs in the Middle East could be settled satisfactorily—guaranteeing the continued flow of the oil—if the United States would change its support-of-Israel policy and respond to the demands of the Arabs. The companies knew that their position in the Middle East was deteriorating rapidly, and at the end they would have to leave the area. But they were determined to utilize the short time left to reap as high profits as possible even at the expense of the United States' national interests, and at the expense of the entire Western world. They hoped that their efforts in influencing American policy against Israel would please the Arab producing countries, and they would reward them by permitting them to continue with the oil exploitation for a little while longer. They tried to assure public opinion that there was no cause for alarm and attempted to discredit those who warned of the oncoming crisis.

Moreover, the extent of the crisis when it came was intentionally exaggerated, which enabled them to increase their profits. They did not plan with Washington on devices to meet the crisis as was done in the 1956 crisis. To be sure, conditions in 1973 were not similar to those of the previous crises in 1956 and 1967; but if the companies

(3) See however the case of Abu Dhabi, chapter VI above page 71.

would have planned with the Administration for the 1973 crisis there could be no doubt that the impact would have been much lighter, and would not have resulted in a general panic.

After carefully examining and analyzing all the aspects of the embargo one arrives at the conclusion that it was not a great success. The only positive result for the producers was the huge increase in the price of oil. The companies came out winners, together with the producers, in reaping huge profits from the high prices, but for them it was a very short-range advantage. In spite of their hopes, their role as concessionaires was systematically and rapidly reduced and was being totally eliminated.

Technically, the embargo was a failure. Were the consuming countries united in their opposition to the producers, and had they made a strong effort to overcome the crisis, the producers would have had to give way. The success of the embargo and of OPEC stemmed, in great measure, from the weakness and hesitations of the consumers. This issue will be dealt with in the next chapter.

Psychologically the embargo gave the Arab producing countries a sense of superiority and importance in both an economic and political sense. It seemed that the world was under their command and ready to do their bidding. The producers succeeded to further fragmentize the already sharply divided and decimated Western camp, when European countries responded to Arab demands in an effort to assure themselves oil supplies. The producers saw all the great and powerful nations competing with one another to sell them the most sophisticated modern weapons including atomic plants. The producers' spokesmen continued to threaten the consuming countries that if they would not comply with the producers' requests, they would face a second embargo.

Let us, therefore, examine the possibilities of the Arab producing countries imposing a second embargo. It should be stressed that the threat of a second embargo was first voiced not by Arab producers, but by the President of the United States and his assistants; and from them the Arab producers took their cue. It would seem that the President's fear of a second embargo was more a tactic against Israel than a realistic appraisal of the situation. In order to "persuade" Israel to agree to the difficult terms of the proposed second separation of forces between Israel and Egypt, the President scared the world by stating that if Israel assumed a rigid position in her negotiations there would be a stalemate created in the Middle East with the attendant danger of a new war. This would bring on a second embargo which would be more harmful and disastrous than the first one.

Let us take a very close look at the facts and study carefully the possibilities of a second embargo. We will assume that the situation will deteriorate, and the efforts at negotiations between the parties will fail and a war will break out. As a move against the consuming countries, the Arab producers will institute a second embargo. We must assume that the United States will continue to support Israel and will supply her with the necessary military and economic aid. Otherwise the possibility of a second embargo would not arise.

The embargo will be imposed on all the Western consuming countries to punish the United States. In a real emergency the United States could well do without Middle East oil. However, those European countries and Japan that depend on the Middle East would have no means for forcing the United States to change her support of Israel. Under such circumstances, the Arab producers would succeed in arousing even greater anger and bitter resentment in the consuming countries—developed and developing—and even move them to concerted action against the Arab countries. The Soviet Union would not be in a position to solve the problems of the Arab countries, and certainly could not meet the needs of the consuming countries.

Under such conditions the great consuming countries would have no alternative but to unite and form one great strong front facing the producers, with the hope of reaching a settlement. The consumers would have learned their lessons from the first embargo, and would be well prepared for the second embargo. Most of the consuming countries would have stockpiled oil supplies for at least three-months' consumption. However, during a prolonged embargo the pressure on such countries as Iraq and Algeria would become too great to withstand, for without the continued oil revenue they could not exist. Nor would Libya endure a prolonged embargo. Iran would no doubt exploit a second embargo as she did the first, and would increase production at the expense of the Arab producers.

External pressure from the consuming countries and internal pressure from some of the producing countries would cause, should a second embargo ever be imposed, a complete break-down of the Arab producers' front, and would endanger OPEC.[4]

---

(4) At the Arab Summit Conference which met in Rabat on October 26-29, 1974, it was reported that the Saudi Arabian Foreign Minister, Omar Saqqaf, warned the conferees that any use of Arab oil as a political weapon at this stage would have disastrous international consequences. At a press conference on November 12, 1975, Henry Kissinger stated that the West would be better prepared to withstand another Arab oil embargo. "An embargo now would have a less sweeping effect" because of the cooperation of the industrialized states. We come, therefore, to the conclusion that from a practical point of view the Arab producers would not risk a second embargo. Some Arab spokesmen have declared that even in case of war there would be no embargo.

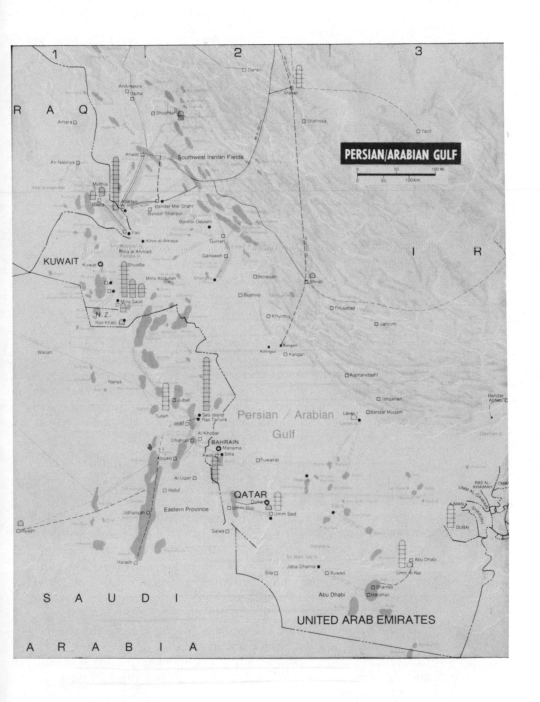

8 The Efforts of the Consuming Countries

It was a well established fact before the outbreak of the October 1973 energy crisis, and even more obvious after the outbreak of the crisis, that most of the Western European countries and Japan were greatly dependent on Middle East oil for the successful functioning and growth of their economies. The energy source whose quantities were large enough, whose production was relatively easy, whose quality was high and access to which was free and unencumbered was available in the Middle East. It was also clear that in spite of the many obstacles and basic difficulties which OPEC experienced in establishing itself, it emerged, ten years after it was organized, as a body strongly united in purpose and adamantly determined to attain its objectives; it was not to be easily deterred by any move or action which the consuming countries might take.

The consuming countries, in contrast were disunited and have not had in the past and have not now a common purpose, and are not ready to resist energetically the demands of the producers. One of the major underlying reasons for this unique phenomenon is the different level of dependence of each group of the consuming countries on Middle East oil.

Although the United States is the greatest consumer of oil in the world, both in absolute quantities and in per capita consumption, her dependence on Middle East oil is very limited. With a relatively easy cut of 10% to 15% in consumption the United States could—even today—free herself, in times of emergency, from any dependence on the Middle East. In spite of her strong determination and effort to continue and even greatly enhance her friendly relations with the Arab producing countries of the Middle East—a determination stemming from economic, political and strategic factors—and her strong desire to improve these relations at the expense of the Soviet Union—detente policy notwithstanding—the United States was willing to adopt bold measures which would free her and the Western countries of economic and political pressures from the Middle East oil producing countries.

The West European countries, in contrast, depended on the Middle East oil for about 68% of their total energy consumption. Although the European Common Market countries were planning to increase, over an extended period of time, their energy supply from local sources, they would remain dependent for most of their energy needs on the Middle East for a long time to come. Japan's situation was even worse. It has been estimated that her dependence on Middle East oil reached as high as 85-90% of her total energy consumption. Since both Western Europe and Japan have no alternative energy sources, they are subject to OPEC pressure.[1]

The economic structures of the three different groups are based on oil energy. The standard of living, the level of industrial development, the technology level, the rate of economic growth, the quality of life and culture are all based on oil energy. Hence the radically different attitude of Japan and Western Europe from that of the United States to the energy problem and to the possible solutions. The United States was never—until the crisis—dependent on energy sources from outside the American Continent, while West European countries were used to dependence on the Middle East and accommodated themselves accordingly. They did not, therefore, suffer from shock at the realization of their dependence, whereas the United States was stunned by the possibility of depending on the Middle East to supply her energy needs—civilian and military, and the threatening implication of such dependence for her global strategy.

Moreover, the Western European countries suffered from a complex dependence on the United States. Throughout the period of oil development the United States had enormous oil resources in her own territory which supplied, for a long time her own needs and she even exported oil to other countries. In addition, she succeeded, since World War I, to gain control of a great part of the oil resources out-

(1) Recently a number of reports appeared in the press that China might become in a number of years one of the great oil producers in the world and would compete with the Middle East oil producing countries. Moreover, Japan would purchase most of her oil from China and would be independent of the Middle East. Indeed, Japan has actually increased her oil purchases from China at the expense of Indonesia, which oil prices, in line with OPEC decisions were higher than those of China. But all the reports about China's future oil possibilities are mere speculation. All the predictions about China's future production and reserves are not based on solid facts, and no reliable information is available about what China's internal energy needs would be and whether she would have any sizable surplus for export. In fact, in spite of the many obstacles and disappointments which Japan had experienced in her efforts of cooperation with some of the Middle Eastern countries, she signed agreements for huge investments, running into hundreds of millions of dollars, in diverse economic undertakings in Middle Eastern countries, especially in Iraq, in return for oil supplies in huge quantities. Thus the Middle Eastern countries seem to remain the major source of oil supplies for Japan —the many predictions and speculations notwithstanding.

side her territory, especially in the Middle East.   Up to the early 'seventies the United States' oil companies possessed the lion's share of all the oil concessions in the Middle East.   The West European countries were, therefore, dependent on American companies for the supply of their oil. They resented, especially France, this humiliating situation and attempted in different ways to extricate themselves from this, to them oppressive, dependence.

When the latest oil crisis broke out and the Arabs imposed an oil embargo primarily on the United States, the West European countries saw a rare occasion to rid themselves of the American yoke.   France saw in the crisis a great opportunity of becoming the new European leader by bringing about a new rapprochement with the Arab Middle East countries and by forging strong and new relations with them. France had an old score to settle with the Anglo-Saxon countries, which she believed were responsible for her elimination from the Middle East.   France envisioned a triumphant return to leadership and high prestige in Europe and in the Arab Middle East.

In line with her tradition, her general national concept and her position in the world, the United States was ready for a match of strength between the producers and the consumers, in which, of course, she would be the leader of the contest. In such a test of strength lurked a danger to her strategic policy in the Middle East, but it was minor, relatively, by comparison to the danger of retreat and surrender to the producing countries. Should the consumers succeed in winning the struggle her prestige would be enhanced as well as that of the entire Western bloc, and she would be strengthened in her global struggle with the Soviet Union. The United States felt strong and ready for battle.

The two basic issues facing all the consuming countries were a continuous and secure supply of oil and reasonable prices for it. On these there was no differences of opinion, but there was a very serious difference of opinion on the steps to be taken to achieve them. Three attempts were made to find a solution for the consumers oil problem, and it would seem, although they are not yet fully completed, that they all failed to solve the energy problem.

The United States was the first to attempt to deal with the oil issue. She believed that the first, decisive and practical step in the contest with the producers must be unification of all the consuming countries into one strong organization which would struggle with the producers. She was convinced that the producers could not withstand a determined united front of the consumers. She expressed this opinion back in 1971 when the efforts of OPEC began to bear fruits of success. However, the West European countries failed to respond.   When

OPEC obtained its demands from the foreign concessionary companies, the United States Under Secretary of State William Casey stated in June 1971 in New York: "We are interested in the development of an effective continuing mechanism among the oil-consuming nations for sharing oil in the event of an emergency curtailment of supply". France, Italy and Japan rejected the proposal. After Libya nationalized the foreign oil companies, especially the American ones, the United States sent a delegation to the Organization for Economic Cooperation and Development (OECD) in Paris and again attempted to persuade the great consuming countries to adopt a program of sharing the oil resources of the participating countries in case of a cut in supplies by the producing countries. However, the European countries steadfastly refused.

After the imposing of the oil embargo in October 1973 by the Arab producers, United States Secretary of State Henry Kissinger called in the middle of December for a cooperative move of the United States, Europe and Japan. He proposed the naming of an energy committee which would be given instructions to prepare a practical program within 90 days. He stressed that the United States would be ready to contribute the major share of the financial and technical needs for the purpose; at a later stage the producing countries would be invited to join this committee.

The President of the United States, Richard Nixon, invited, on January 9, 1974, the foreign ministers of France, Britain, West Germany, Italy, Holland, Norway, Canada and Japan to a conference in Washington to meet on February 11, to deal with the energy crisis which resulted from the Arab oil embargo. This invitation caused internal difficulties in the European Common Market. At a meeting of the Foreign Ministers of the Market which took place in Brussels, four days after the Nixon invitation, France attempted to block the United States efforts. Accepting the United States invitation would have interfered with her objective which she achieved. (The November 6, 1973 declaration) out of which she hoped to develop friendly relations with the Arab countries. However, on January 15, the members of the Common Market—very strenuous French objections notwithstanding—decided to accept the Nixon invitation. France tried thereupon to persuade the Market members who would attend, that the conference should not go beyond the formulation of general principles on the question of energy, that under no circumstances should it deal with tactics and measures against the producing countries.

The conference opened as scheduled with a speech by the U.S. Secretary of State, host of the conference; in it he presented a seven-point program, and he proposed the creation of a new body to deal with the energy problem. In spite of France's objection the conference adopted the Kissinger plan and decided to appoint a coordinating committee which would prepare a program for a conference of consumers and producers, which was to be convened at the earliest possible date.

Two weeks after the conclusion of the Washington conference representatives of the 12 countries—8 members of the Common Market (France refused to join), Canada, Japan, Norway and the United States—met in Washington to form the coordinating committee. The reaction of the producers was not late in coming. The Secretary General of OPEC attacked the conference and maintained, as did France, that the proper forum for dealing with the energy question was the United Nations. Arab spokesmen described the conference and its decisions as provocation aimed at a confrontation between producers and consumers. Since, however, the consumers were not deterred by the opposition of the producers and of France, the political commentators at the time saw in the conference and its decisions an impressive diplomatic victory for the United States.

The 7-member coordinating committee met in Brussels on March 13, and decided to establish three special sub-committees: one to formulate the role of the international oil companies, one to examine the state of research in the conventional sources of energy, and one to deal with atomic energy. The committee itself continued to deal with the energy crisis; on August 5, it formulated a two-paragraph agreement. In case of a new embargo against one of the member countries, the others would see it as aimed at all of them and they would share their energy resources with the embargoed member. The member states were to regulate their oil price and supply policies in such a fashion as not to disturb industrial development and economic prosperity. The committee also decided that members which are also producers should increase output, and that all members were to enlarge their oil stockpiles in order to be prepared in case of a second embargo.[2]

On October 30, Belgium, which acted as temporary secretary of the coordinating committee, announced that the United States and 9 other countries had decided to establish the International Energy Agency. It would be officially inaugurated in Paris on November 18, and would be an autonomous body within the OECD framework.

(2) According to the *New York Times*, the coordinating committee adopted a secret decision on September 19 to establish an international energy agency whose purpose would be to oppose the producers. The official announcement was to be made in November.

Six other countries: Austria, Switzerland, *Sweden* Spain, Australia and New Zealand indicated that they would join.[3]

In an attempt, apparently, to obtain maximum results from the efforts of the coordinating committee the U.S. Secretary of State asked the Foreign and Finance Ministers of France, Britain, West Germany and Japan to a special conclave at Camp David, at the end of September, to deal with the energy problem. After the discussions no decisions were made public. It was also reported, however, that very serious differences of opinion emerged. It was reported that one of the decisions adopted was to take measures to reduce energy consumption by 15%. It was generally believed that such a cut in consumption would inevitably reduce the price of oil.

The establishment of the International Energy Agency was formally announced on November 18. In addition to the general organizational structure and the system of voting, the Agency took the following decisions: a 10-year blueprint was to be worked out which would reduce the dependence on imported oil by limiting demand and by developing alternatives; the major role of the Agency was defined as coordinating all the energy measures of the consuming countries, including sharing energy sources in times of emergency.[4]

In spite of the enthusiasm at the time of the founding of the Agency and the readiness of many more countries to join the new organization, it was obvious that the conflicting interests of the members, and especially those of the United States and Western Europe and Japan, were deep and wide and would not suddenly disappear merely because of the establishment of a new international body. The Western European countries and Japan were not ready to adopt measures that would lead to an open contest between themselves and the producing countries. They believed that they could attain the desired ends without resorting to extremes.

For three days the IEA met in Paris in the first week of February 1975 and dealt with three issues: (1) Kissinger's proposal to establish a floor price of $7 per barrel of oil in order to induce investors to develop alternatives to Middle East oil; (2) the topics of discussion of the preliminary conference and later the conference of consumers and producers; (3) the date for the preliminary conference and agenda of the conference.

The Agency did not adopt, at the time, the Kissinger proposal; the

---

(3) On the same day, the French Premier, Jacques Chirac, repeated that his country refused to join a bloc of consuming countries. He added: "France's policy has not changed. The price increases of raw materials are legitimate. France refuses to be part of a confrontation between users and sellers".

(4) By the end of December 1974, Spain, Turkey, Austria, Switzerland and Sweden joined the agency.

subject of discussion of the proposed conference was to be limited to oil, and the conference date was set for March. However, the American representative declared that the adoption of the Kissinger proposal was a prerequisite for convening the conference in March.

Before we continue with the story of the IEA and the efforts of France to change its objectives, we should deal with a parallel development in the relations between the European Common Market countries and the Arab League countries.

Under the leadership of France the Common Market Countries issued on November 6, 1973—after the proclamation of the embargo —a pro-Arab declaration. At a secret meeting of the foreign ministers of the Market which took place in Copenhagen on December 14, 1973 it was unanimously decided to propose a basic program of cooperation and mutual assistance between the members of the Market and between the Arab League countries. The former were to supply the necessary financial resources and assist in the economic development of the latter, while the latter were to guarantee steady supplies of oil at stable prices to the former.[5]

At the end of January 1974 when the Foreign Ministers of the Market met in Brussels, France tried to convince her colleagues that the United States proposal to organize the consuming countries was dangerous and would affect adversely European vital interests, which the United States did not risk, for she was not dependent on Middle East oil. After much effort by France, the West German Foreign Minister, who was the rotating chairman of the Market Council, announced that it was decided to open a dialogue with the Arab countries. The United States was disturbed by this decision, especially since she was concentrating, at the time, all her efforts on the consumers' conference and was deeply involved in the separation of forces agreements between Israel and her neighbors. The Market decision could only upset and even defeat the efforts of the United States. Indeed, in a letter to Willy Brandt, West German Chancellor, President Nixon criticized the Market decision and saw it as an anti-American move. Some members of the Market were also disturbed by the decision; it was reported that Britain objected to the dialogue.

The form of the dialogue was formulated as an examination of the possibilities of cooperation in the areas of energy, economics and technology. However, serious differences of opinion broke out when

(5) On September 4, 1973, after Libya nationalized 51% of the foreign oil companies operating in her territory, the Premier, Major Abdul Salam Jallud stated that the suggestions that the United States could force the European Common Market countries not to buy nationalized oil in Libya were out of the question. "Libya is ready to coopeaate with Europe for mutual advantage in forging a new and natural partnership based on Arab oil and European technology".

the Foreign Ministers of the Market convened in Luxembourg early in May. All the participants agreed, in principle, to the dialogue, including Britain, but the latter proposed continuous consultation with the United States on the issue of the dialogue. France, of course, objected; Britain thereupon made consultation with the United States a condition against using her veto. The issue reached a stalemate.

However, at the NATO conference in June, Kissinger announced that his government no longer objected to the dialogue. But the internal Market objection still persisted. For in spite of the lifting of the oil embargo against the United States and most of the European countries in March, the embargo was still in force against Holland, and she objected to the dialogue as long as the embargo against her continued. By the end of July, when the embargo against Holland was lifted, the French Foreign Minister, as rotating chairman, began negotiating for the dialogue. Britain insisted that the dialogue must not involve political issues, while France stressed the need for cooperation by both sides. The political secretariat of the Market prepared a "secret" document and the Foreign Ministers were required to abide by its guidelines in the negotiations.

The topics for discussion were: science, technology, meteorology, ecology problems and education. The date for the first meeting of the two sides was set for July 31, 1974. The participants for the Market were the French Foreign Minister and the Chairman of the Market Commission, and for the Arab League the Secretary General and the Kuwaiti Foreign Minister. It should be noted that from the very beginning when the dialogue proposal was broached the great Arab oil producing countries displayed no particular interest in it. They apparently preferred their own bi-lateral negotiations and agreements for cooperation with the individual European countries, especially when their treasuries were bursting with money, and the means of cooperation at their command and under their own control. They were not interested in becoming involved in the plans of all the Arab non-producing countries.

The attempt on the part of the Market to limit the discussions to economic questions and not become involved in the current political issues of the Arab countries failed from the outset, and caused embarrassment to the main negotiator, France. The Kuwaiti Foreign Minister, one of the two Arab League representatives declared that it was impossible to separate economics from politics, and the League Secretary General supported him by pointing out that the very discussions were conducted within a political framework (Arab League).

The two delegations decided to establish permanent mixed committees which were to prepare long-range programs for cooperation of the two sides. Meanwhile the two sides would continue to try to establish principles for cooperation and set up a system of priorities and joint projects.

After the political committee of the Arab League heard a report of the progress of the discussions from the Secretary General, it authorized him and the Lebanese Foreign Minister to continue with the negotiations scheduled to resume on October 20 in Paris. Meanwhile representatives of both sides met in Cairo to prepare the agenda for the Paris meeting. However, when the Paris meeting opened in November, a month later than scheduled, serious difficulties developed, and it was reported that the discussions reached a stalemate. The major issue was the opposition of a number of Market countries to the participation of the Palestine Liberation Organization (PLO) as a full member of the Arab League. They insisted that representation of both the Market and the League must be by fully sovereign countries. France favored PLO participation, but others persistently objected.

On April 22, 1975, the Arab League authorized its representatives to proceed with the dialogue. On the issue of PLO representation a compromise was worked out. The delegations would not be based on countries, but on the Market as a whole and the League as a whole. The latter could include, should it so desire, a PLO representative on its delegation.

On July 22 a conference for advancing the dialogue between Europe and the Arab world was opened in Rome. The 150 delegates were non-governmental specialists from the nine members of the Market and from 21 Arab League delegations. Topics discussed were: economics, finances, technology, culture and social affairs. Ironically, because of Arab objection, oil—the very reason for the dialogue—was not included in the agenda.

The third round of discussions took place in November 22-27 at Abu Dhabi, and was attended by some 100 experts from both sides. The stumbling block to progress was a difference of opinion regarding the political issues in the Middle East. A press statement at the conclusion of the meeting said: "The two sides announce that the political aspect of the dialogue must be taken into consideration to allow the dialogue to make progress in an effective manner conducive to the fulfillment of its aims."

However, the official negotiations between the Market and the League made no progress. In spite of the compromise on the PLO representation, the Arabs insisted on full recognition of the PLO. It would seem that with the advance of the status of the PLO in the international forums, the League disregarded the compromise and demanded full official recognition of the PLO by the Market countries.

The relations between the Market and the League were based on the pro-Arab Market declaration of November 6, 1973 which was adopted after efforts by France, as mentioned above. In order to make it possible to give the PLO full recognition and all that such recognition would imply, a number of Market members tried to introduce an addendum to the declaration, which would give full support to PLO. While France strongly advocated the adoption of the new addition, and was even reportedly supported by England and West Germany, others objected not only to the proposed addendum but to the very raising of the issue for discussion. The League, however, insisted on full recognition. The deadlock continued.

The nine Market foreign ministers met in Luxembourg on February 25, 1976 and approved the next stage in the dialogue which was to open in May. Although the stress was still to be on the same subjects, the Market was willing to include also political issues for discussion. When the meeting opened on May 19 in Luxembourg, the League Secretary General devoted most of his statement to the practical issues of cooperation between the two sides, but the other delegate, the Foreign Minister of Bahrain, devoted his entire statement to the question of the Palestinians. The atmosphere became tense, and the meeting adjourned for a day. In the meantime France attempted to persuade the other members of the Market to adopt the addendum, but without success. The issue was not resolved.

As a countermove to the American effort in organizing the oil consuming countries into a solid bloc whose major objective was to meet with the producers and struggle with them, the Saudi Arabian oil minister Yamani proposed in April 1974, at the special sixth session of the United Nations General Assembly, and before that on other occasions, to stage a dialogue between the producers and consumers, before the latter consolidated themselves into a firm and united organized bloc. He suggested that the dialogue be between three groups of countries: producers—Iran, Algeria, Saudi Arabia and Venezuela; consumers—United States, the European Common Market countries, and Japan; developing countries—India, Brazil and Zaire. His aim was obvious. By widening the framework of the participants he aimed at guaranteeing a majority for the producers. For on every issue and on any question that would come up the developing countires would side with the producers. Moreover, since of the three groups the producers were the best organized with clearly defined objectives and had a distinct plan of action, whereas the other two groups were disunited and had no well-defined aims, the producers would be in total control. Should the Saudi Arabian proposal be accepted, the IEA would be weakened and its objectives blurred even more.

Now, France, which strenuously objected to the United States efforts, jumped on the Yamani proposal and adopted it as her own. Her initiative in sponsoring the plan would gain for her prestige and influence among all the three groups. On October 24, 1974 the French President Valery Giscard d'Estaing proposed to convene a conference composed of representatives of the oil producing countries, the oil consuming countries and the developing countries to deal with economic and financial questions. France then began to press for convening the conference early in 1975, and proposed 12 countries which would represent the three groups. In November 1974 she informed her colleagues in the Market, the United States, Japan, Saudi Arabia and Algeria of her plans.[6]

In the middle of December it was reported that most of the producers of the Persian Gulf area, Egypt and the Arab League supported the French plan, but the United States vigorously opposed it. She maintained that the planned conference could be convened only after the consuming countries to participate in it organized and adopted a united plan of action. A deadlock developed. However, at a summit conference between the President of France and the President of the United States on the island of Martinique on December 14-16, the two arrived at some vague and obscure compromise, which made it possible for France to continue with her efforts. It was agreed to convene in March in Paris a preliminary meeting of the representatives of the producers and consumers to prepare the agenda for the conference.[7] On March 2, 1975, the President of France sent out invitations to 10 countries for the preparatory conference to be held on April 7 in Paris.

In the meantime, the conference of the developing countries which convened in Dakar February 4-8 to deal with the over-all question of raw materials decided that the negotiations between the oil producing and oil consuming countries be expanded to include other raw materials. The main leader at the Dakar conference was Algeria, and she had her own reasons for demanding the widening of the scope of the proposed conference. The United States on the other side was determinedly opposed to the expansion of the conference.

The preparatory conference was opened in Paris on April 7. After prolonged and difficult discussions and debates lasting 9 days the conference broke up without arriving at any decision. The United States persisted that the discussions be limited to the question of energy, while Algeria equally persisted that other raw materials be

(6) On October 24 when the French President made his proposal he said: "This idea, incidentally, has been mooted by others apart from us. For example, it has been proposed on several occasions by Saudi Arabia".

(7) The compromise arrived at was apparently expressed in the decision of the Presidents that "the preparatory discussions will be followed by intensive consultations among consumer countries in order to prepare positions for the conference".

included. The break-up of the preparatory conference was considered at the time as a serious defeat for the French effort. But France was not ready to give up her plan and pursued her objective relentlessly. After a while the United States softened her position. At the United Nations General Assembly Secretary of State Kissinger proposed a compromise which would make possible the resumption of the work of the preparatory conference. He proposed the naming of separate but parallel commissions for energy, raw materials, development and finances. The European Common Market Commission supported the Kissinger compromise proposal.

France, therefore, announced on September 30 that the 10 countries which were invited to the preparatory conference responded favorably to the invitation, and that the conference would meet in Paris on October 13. Its major purpose was to organize a world summit conference to deal with the question of energy and other raw materials, it was to name the 27 countries which would participate in the full conference, it would prepare the agenda and establish the commissions which would begin negotiations in December.

As planned the preparatory conference opened on October 13. However, basic differences of opinion appeared on the question of guidelines for the four commissions. The developing countries, which hoped that the conference would bring about revolutionary changes in the world economic order, demanded that the instructions to the commissions be specific and detailed, and on the basis of these instructions the commissions would prepare practical recommendations which would be binding on the conference. The industrialized nations on the other hand, which were not ready to change the world economic structure, demanded that the commissions be given full freedom in their choice of recommendations without committing in advance the conference and its participants. The United States came forward with some sort of a compromise; she proposed that the preparatory conference adopt the nonspecific, vaguely defined functions of the commission as formulated in Paris, but to them be attached the various interpretations given these functions by the participants.

On October 16, the 10 delegations completed their discussion, made public a general declaration and decided to convene the conference on December 16 in Paris. The full conference was to be composed of 27 countries; of these, 19 were developing nations—among them oil producers—and 8 were industrialized countries. The four commissions were not given specific instructions.[8]

(8) A new crisis potentially capable of exploding the conference broke out when Britain requested separate representation. In view of her role as a future major oil producer, she felt that she would be inadequately represented by the Common Market delegate (in reality France). However, on December 3, it was announced in London that Britain gave up her demand, and the road was cleared for the conference.

The conference was duly opened in Paris on December 16, and its official name was the International Conference for Economic Cooperation, while the popular name was the North-South Dialogue. The President of France, as host, delivered the opening speech, and he stressed the importance of the conference. He declared that historically the conference was of no less significance than the founding of the United Nations. The major idea behind the United Nations was the establishment of a new world political order, the Paris conference was to establish a new world economic order. The French did not hide their glee at the achievement of the opening of the conference, and saw in it a great French diplomatic victory.

But the central figure of the conference was no doubt the United States Secretary of State. It was reported that he told correspondents flying in the plane with the American delegation to Paris that the United States aid to the developing countries would be halted if they would continue to back the oil producers' policies. At the conference Kissinger minced no words in warning the producers by declaring that "higher oil prices would seriously impair the economic recovery, would hamper international trade and increase the internal difficulties of many countries." Moreover, "as a result of the higher prices the ability of the developed countries to aid the developing countries would be weakened, and the pattern of international cooperation would be harmed." His speech was a direct attack on the oil producers' policies.

Britain intervened in the discussion when Foreign Secretary James Callaghan pressed for the establishment of a floor price for oil in order to protect British investment in developing its North Sea oil resources.

The clash involving the United States, Britain and France was more than obvious, and it did not bode well for the hopes and aims of the conference. France assailed Britain's intervention as the French President declared that it did not conform with the joint Common Market position worked out at the EEC summit talks in Rome.

The producing countries reacted very strongly to Kissinger's harsh words. They rejected out of hand the assertion that the rise in oil prices caused the world inflation and the world economic crisis. The Algerian Foreign Minister Abdelaziz Bouteflika said: "It is unjust to turn notorious non-truths into truths". The Iranian delegate stated that "The West's recession has been wholly homemade". They demanded that the price of all natural resources be based on an index of the prices of products which the developing countries purchase from the industrialized nations. The latter refused to base the prices of the natural resources, especially oil, on an index.

The conference, however, proceeded and chairmen were named for the four commissions. The United States and Saudi Arabia were elected co-chairman of the energy commission. The four commissions were established and another preparatory meeting was scheduled for January 26, 1976. The commissions were to begin their work on February 11, and they were to report back to the conference to be convened about February 1977. Even though the industrialized countries prevailed, and no specific instructions were given to the commissions, the developing countries demanded that the issues be taken up again at the preparatory meeting on January 26. Indeed, representatives of the 19 developing countries met on January 5 in Paris and dealt with the issue of negotiations between themselves and the 8 developed countries, and drafted specific instructions to be given to the commissions.

On February 11, the conference met with the two major issues —indexation and instructions to the commissions—unresolved.

The commissions under the guidance of the co-chairmen of the Conference, Allan MacEachen, Canadian External Minister, and Manuel Perez Guerrero, Venezuelan Minister of State, were wrestling with the issues assigned to them. But by July 1976, the bargaining between the two sides broke down. After patient efforts of two months, the co-chairmen succeeded to work out a compromise formula to resume the negotiations. The two major issues were the heavy debts of the Third World countries, and a guarantee of the purchasing power of the producers of oil and other raw materials against world inflation.

The commissions met in private in September, October and November with the aim of convening the Conference in the middle of December.

While the OPEC conference was approaching, an attempt was apparently made to link the level of the oil increase to the results of the Conference. The United States, which was the major power to deal with the two questions, resisted the pressure. Secretary of State Henry Kissinger sent a cable early in December to the European negotiators and warned them of the dangers in establishing a direct link between any concessions offered developing countries in the Paris dialogue and price moderation by oil exporting countries at their meeting in Qatar. He declared: "We are convinced that there is no negotiable CIEC package which the industrialized countries could accept and which would also present sufficient inducement to OPEC to refrain from a substantial oil price increase over several years, given the lack of leverage by consumers over oil prices."

The conference meeting scheduled to open December 15, was postponed by the United States' initiative to the following spring.

We may now return to IEA. At the end of May 1975 it adopted a program aimed at attaining its objectives. Some of the measures included a cut in consumption of 2 million barrels a day, cooperation among the consumers by establishing, through a revolving fund, a $25 billion "safety net" for granting loans to members of the Agency for the purchase of oil, and agreement on a minimum floor price for oil. Members approved a plan for cooperation in the development of alternatives for oil, which would involve huge investments of funds, and development of sophisticated technologies.

From the above pages it is obvious that the first energetic efforts of the United States to organize a united solid bloc against OPEC and stand up to the producing countries in order to guarantee a steady supply of oil at reasonable prices was weak and nearly bereft of meaning, and in its place the oil producing countries—with the help of France—attempted, through the International Conference for Economic Cooperation, to exploit the situation for their benefit. The European Common Market-Arab League dialogue, through which France hoped to reenter the Middle East by some mutual understanding with the Arabs, was turned into political struggle for the recognition of the PLO. The efforts of France to convert the IEA into some sort of "poly-alogue" among three groups of countries, producers, consumers and developing countries, was reduced by Algeria, not without French help, into a struggle between the industrialized and developing countries that owned raw materials. The main purpose: resistence of the domination of the oil producing countries, and the total elimination of high oil prices. After almost 3 years since the outbreak of the energy crisis, the consumers stand helpless in spite of the strong and threatening warnings of the United States which were made from time to time against the producing countries and their supporters.

In the struggle between the producers and the consumers the weakness and helplessness of the latter was amply demonstrated. All the daring efforts of the United States and the very modest efforts of France were doomed to fail for they lacked the proper motivation for a united determined stand of the consumers, and a readiness to take the proper measures for the realization of the objectives. They all worked at cross purposes, each trying to advance its own interests at the expense of the others. At the end the United States gave in and did not live up to her threats.

9 Surpluses and Recycling

After the problem of securing oil supplies, the consuming countries were preoccupied with the huge monetary surpluses which have been accumulating in the treasuries of the producing countries. The high prices which the consuming countries were forced to pay for their imported oil have caused immense deficits in their balance of payments. These countries were compelled to devote a great portion of their national resources to cover the import cost of the oil. But these resources did not return to them in the form of purchases for their products or as investments in their economies. They remained as surpluses in the treasuries of the producing countries. The outcome: lower standard of living, unemployment and general chaotic conditions in the economic and financial structures.

The question of the monetary surpluses was directly related to the price level. Many experts sought to justify the steep increases in the oil price by maintaining that the oil companies refused, over a long period of time, to raise the oil prices while the prices of other products went up constantly. This argument is specious, for oil prices began to rise some twelve years ago. They began to climb, relatively slowly at first to be sure, but steadily since 1965. The direct oil revenue of the producing countries continuously and very substantially expanded, not at the expense of the companies, but at the expense of the consuming public.[1]

However, since October 1973, the oil price rose very highly and rapidly. Early in 1974, oil prices increased four-fold over what they were in September 1973, and since then the royalties and profit share of the producers went up steeply. In October 1975, oil prices went up again by 10% and in December 1976 increased again 5%-10%. As a result of these increases the question of the monetary surpluses became more acute and so did the problem of the balance of payments deficits. The producing countries have accumulated much greater surpluses

(1) The Saudi Arabian Monetary Agency's *Annual Report* for 1975 produced a table which shows that the price of Arabian light crude oil went up by 70% between January 1971 and June 1, 1973, and the Government revenue per barrel almost doubled.

than the totals which they received only a few years previously. If the producers were not to return their revenue in purchases of products, in investments or in the form of loans, a great number of the consuming countries would not be able to pay for their new oil purchases.

The Middle East oil producing countries fall into two different groups in terms of utilizing the oil revenues which flow into their treasuries. One includes Iran, Iraq and Algeria; they all have wide and very ambitious large scale development programs. All are in great need of large financial resources to fund their development projects which grow more stupendously from year to year. Their surpluses, after all expenses and payments are deducted, are either relatively small or non-existent. Iran's recent government budget showed a serious deficit. The other group consists of Saudi Arabia, Kuwait, Libya and the Persian Gulf Amirates; their populations are sparse, and their development plans are comparatively limited. They are not in need of very large incomes; since their revenues are huge they accumulate gigantic surpluses.

What did the producing countries do with their surpluses? Before we attempt to answer this question, we should perhaps deal with the magnitude of the surpluses.

Back in the middle of 1973 a senior New York bank specialist estimated that by the end of the 'seventies the Middle East producers would accumulate a surplus of $175 billion—the greatest money accumulation that was ever amassed in the history of world commerce. The same banker estimated that at the end of the decade the U. S. balance of payments deficit would have reached $21 billion, that of Western Europe $25 billion and that of Japan $15 billion. According to that estimate the annual revenue of the oil producing countries of the Middle East would have reached $30 to $40 billion, out of which Saudi Arabia would have received $20 billion. Even at that time the pressure of the Middle East surpluses was being felt on the international money markets especially in West Germany, a pressure which caused occasional closing of the great stock exchanges in Europe in order to prevent a run on the U.S. dollar. A special report of OECD warned then of the possibility of danger to the monetary markets from the accumulated financial power in the hands of the oil producing countries.

These forecasts were dwarfed by the actual developments in a very short period of time. After the Arab oil embargo at the end of 1973 and the steep rapid climb of oil prices which followed the embargo, the producers' surpluses increased dramatically and the dangers stemming from the surpluses became even more menacing.

A secret study conducted in the middle of 1974 by the International

Bank concluded that by 1980 the oil producers' surplus would reach $650 billion, and in 1985 might reach $1,200 billion. This amount was ten times larger than all the United States investments in foreign countries, and a hundred times larger than all the gold held by the United States. Another study conducted by the economic specialists of the European Common Market concluded that if the oil prices were to remain stable, if oil consumption in Western Europe were to be drastically curtailed, and if the hopes for producers' investments in Europe were to be fully realized, the balance of payments deficit of five Market countries—Italy, Britain, France, Denmark and Ireland—would reach $90 billion in 1978.

The best and most efficient way to solve the economic and financial problems which were created by the oil crisis would have been to lower oil prices. A certain reduction—no one would think of bringing them back to what they were before the crisis broke out—would strengthen the economic structures of the consuming countries, would stabilize the monetary structures, would reduce the huge surpluses in the hands of the producers and the dangers that would stem from them and would reduce considerably the deficit of the balance of payments of the consuming countries. In order to achieve this objective the consuming countries would have to be ready to adopt special drastic measures commensurate with the threatening conditions. They would have to cooperate and act as one consolidated bloc, and would have to be prepared for a show-down and a long and determined struggle with the producers.

However, the consuming countries have displayed neither the readiness nor the will for such a struggle. Most of them seem to have despaired of reducing oil prices by bringing pressure on the producers; they have reconciled themselves—out of various calculations and motivations stemming from the economic and political relations between themselves—to the high oil prices. But they were disturbed by the balance of payments deficits, and busied themselves with various schemes and devices to recycle the producers' dollars.

Specialists of international economics assumed that in one form or another the producing countries would have to return their surpluses to the consumers. Otherwise, their surpluses lying in their treasuries would do them no good. According to this assumption, the producers would utilize their surpluses in acquiring additional products and services from the consuming countries, in investing them or in granting them as loans on profitable terms. In other words, theoretically it might be assumed that the surpluses would be recycled to the consuming countries, and on a global basis a balance would be established between producers and consumers. Even with this optimistic forecast, the specialists were concerned (and with them no doubt the governments of the consuming countries) with the question of which countries the producers would choose to invest or grant loans. The producing countries seem to have been guided by purely economic-financial considerations in deciding on the investments and the loans. They have preferred to invest their funds in the great and developed countries, in order to insure both the capital and the expectant returns from the investments and the loans. They certainly would not invest in the weak industrialized countries, such as Italy, and most assuredly not in the developing countries. The result would be that the countries desperately in need of investments and loans would not benefit from the great surpluses of the oil producing countries, and their inability to pay for their oil purchases would become a matter of their very existence. The poor countries of Asia, Africa and South America suffered more than the others from the high oil prices. The sums which the developing countries paid for the oil in 1974 amounted to about $10 billion, and all the assistance they received for their economic development from the industrialized countries totalled $11.4 billion. This meant that practically all the aid was spent for the oil, and very little was left for economic development.

When OPEC decided at the end of September 1975 to increase the price of oil by 10% the international finance specialists calculated that the price increment would cost the oil consuming countries an additional $10 billion annually. Europe would have to pay an extra $5 billion, Japan $1.2 billion, the United States $2 billion, and the developing countries about $1.5 billion. The December 1976 increase would add another extra $11 billion.

The great developed consuming countries decided, therefore, to search for means of persuading the producing countries to transfer a part of their surpluses to the weaker and developing nations. To achieve this end the United States (the Kissinger plan), the International Bank (especially through the International Monetary Fund) and OECD sought to develop new technical instrumentalities for transferring the surpluses to the consuming countries which needed them most. All the experts agreed that the existing mechanisms were incapable of solving the surplus problem and that it was necessary to establish new ones.

However, is the problem of transferring the huge surpluses from the producers to the consumers merely a technical one? The vast revenue which they received for their oil and the huge surpluses which they have amassed gave the producers enormous economic and financial power which resulted in political influence. They would not be ready, of their own free will, to surrender this power and the resultant influence. Practically all the producing countries shared a deep and bitter feeling that the foreign oil companies and their home governments exploited them for many years, oppressed their peoples and controlled them. They firmly believed that the consuming countries have prevented them from playing their proper roles in the international arena, roles to which they were entitled because of their tremendous oil resources; and they were prevented from exerting their due influence on the political and economic development of the community of nations. All because of the political oppression and the economic exploitation of their countries. For the oil companies had all the advantages: technical knowledge, financial resources and political power, while they, the producers, were forced to comply with all demands and conditions imposed upon them by the foreign oil companies. Now the wheel of fortune had turned; they, the producers, are in control. They could stop the flow of the oil any time they so desired without fearing the reaction of the consuming countries; they set the oil prices and they have the financial resources which they could utilize to exploit the consuming countries as the latter had exploited the producing countries in former days. Indeed, all the great and powerful industrialized countries are competing with one another to benefit from the producers' immense financial resources.

Under such psychological conditions it should not be expected that the producers would be ready to surrender their newly won power, and fall in line with the new technical devices for recycling the petro-dollars, through mechanisms which the financial experts of the consuming countries were devising. In fact, the experts who prepared these new devices admit that as long as the psychological obstacle existed, it would not be possible to activate the old and the new mechanisms for solving the surpluses problem. However, not one expert had as yet discovered a way of overcoming the psychological stumbling block.

To concretize the magnitude of the revenue of the producers, the London *Economist* calculated the possible acquirements which OPEC countries could obtain with their oil income. They could buy the shares of all the companies registered in the world big stock exchanges within 15.6 years; all the shares of the companies registered in the New York Stock Exchanges in 9.2 years; all the gold in the central banks of the world in 3.2 years; all the United States' investments abroad in 1.8 years; all the shares of the companies registered in the stock exchanges of France, England and West Germany in 1.7 years; all the IBM shares in 143 days; all the shares of the big American oil company, EXXON in 79 days. Finally the writer mentioned the fact that Kuwait alone acquired 14% of the shares of the West German motor car company Daimler-Benz for a sum equal to her oil revenue of 15 days.

It should be emphasized that we do not have exact figures of the oil revenue of the producing countries, nor of the extent of their investments and the loans they granted, nor of the proportions of the surpluses. All the figures that have been publicized are mere estimates or educated guesses. Nevertheless, it is comparatively much easier to estimate the revenue than the scope of their investments and their monetary surpluses.

Let us examine the year 1974. The estimates of the revenue were given as between $90 and $110 billion. The net surpluses which remained in the hands of the producers, after deducting all current expenses, development projects and various purchases of goods and services, were estimated as between $55 and $65 billion. The chairman of the Federal Reserve Bank, Arthur Burns, estimated that the producers' investments totalled $27 billion; about $16.5 billion were invested in Europe, and about $10.5 billion in the United States. The last amount included the purchase of United States Government Bonds in the amount of $5 billion. In the same year the deficit in the balance of payments of the consuming countries—developed and developing—amounted to $67 billion. The share of the poor developing countries in this total was $26 billion, of Europe $23.8 billion and of the United States $9.5.

Granted that these figures are far from accurate, it is nevertheless obvious that the total deficit in the balance of payments of the consuming countries is more or less equal to the surpluses in the hands of the producing countries. Of course, there were other factors besides the oil prices which caused the deficit, especially in the case of the developing countries but one can not escape the conclusion that the steep increase in oil prices was the major if not the decisive cause for the enormous deficit in the balance of payments, more than three times what it was in 1973.

The oil producing countries do not rush to invest in long term undertakings: they are interested in good safe deals of short duration. They prefer to sink their monies in profitable projects over which they could exert influence and even gain control—their frequent denials of such intentions notwithstanding—both economic-financial and political. From what is known it is clear that they are interested primarily, naturally enough, in all the branches of the oil industry, from exploration through retail marketing, after which they seek basic economic industries in the economies of the consuming countries. Iran, for instance, tried to gain control of the refining and marketing branches of the oil industry in Italy. But the terms she demanded were so harsh that Italy rejected the offer. Iran also attempted to penetrate the oil retail and marketing industry in the United States. She acquired about 25% of the steel division of the German Krupp Company, and bought 13% of the shares of the Pan American Aviation Company.

An Arab company tried to acquire 40% of the American Lockheed Company for about $100 million. The company accepted, at first, the offer but later retreated. The Arabs blamed the United States government for the company's rejection of the offer. Kuwait, as mentioned above, obtained 14% of the shares of the Daimler-Benz automobile manufacturing company.

The governments of various Arab countries have acquired large portions of real estate companies, owners of famous giant buildings in Britain, France and the United States. Many attempts were made— some successfully—to buy a number of banks in the United States, especially in the country towns. Arab capitalists have tried to buy great coal mines in Pennsylvania. The prices offered were inflated and the mine owners were ready to sell.

Because of the high deficits in the balance of payments and because of the desire to increase business, many consuming countries were anxious for new undertakings and encouraged all sorts of investments by the producers in their countries. But as they realized that the producers might control the undertakings in which they were investing they began to prepare legislation which would limit foreign investments in basic industries. Such legislation, however, whether motivated by economic or security considerations, would be a double edged sword. While it might prevent foreigners from gaining control of vital economic and security concerns, it would, at the same time, stem the flow of the petro-dollars which the consuming countries were so anxious to obtain. It would also evoke counter-legislation which would ban the investment of the consuming countries in the developing world. Such legislation would be a heavy blow which might cause total collapse of international trade and the international monetary structure which is very delicate and fragile as it is.

The consuming countries, therefore, found themselves between the devil and the deep blue sea. Should they permit the producers to invest their surpluses in the basic industries of the consumers, they might gain control of those industries and acquire dangerous influence over the consumers economies. Should they refuse the investments, the balance of payments deficits would grow ever larger and would endanger the financial structure.

It would stand to reason that the producing countries should hesitate to invest in the consuming countries basic industries in order to gain control of them. For the consuming countries might take a page from the history of the producers and nationalize those industries, as they, the producers, did to the Western oil companies. Theoretically, this fear would be a sufficient deterrent to prevent the producing countries from attempting to gain control of the basic industries of the consuming countries, and thus stabilize the investment process without endangering the consuming countries' economies. However, a closer examination might reveal that the danger of nationalization might not be a sufficient deterrent for the producing countries. For they would have a powerful counter-weapon against nationalization, they could stop the flow of the oil to the countries which would nationalize the undertakings in which they would have gained control.

The huge surpluses in the hands of the producers which are neither invested nor granted as loans, give the producers a very dangerous monetary and economic weapon against the consuming countries. The producers, especially the big and rich ones, are in a position to flood the international money markets with the currency of a consuming country or countries and thus undermine the monetary value of that country or countries. They might also refuse to accept as payment for the oil the currency of a certain country, thus not only endangering the currency value but the very economic structure of these countries.[2]

In discussing the various weapons of the Arab producers against the consumers, the Saudi Arabian Oil Minister at the end of August 1976 stated that the use of the money weapon by the producers would not be as successful as the oil weapon unless there were changes in the international monetary system and Arab financial institutions were established to give the Arabs greater international influence. He declared that "just as the oil weapon was ineffective in 1967 because it was not ready for use, so the money weapon will be ineffective if we use it prematurely."

In the last year or so a number of financial specialists have questioned some of the assumptions in the descriptions of the oil crisis. A number of international economic experts stressed the fact that the

(2) In March 1976 the United States Treasury revealed that the members of OPEC bought various stocks and bonds in the United States during 1975 amounting to $1.4 billion, compared to $363 million in 1974, a three-fold increase; in addition they purchased $4.8 billions worth of United States Government Bonds. OPEC members' investments in Britain, on the other hand, amounted in 1975 to $250 million compared to $7.5 billion in 1974. London reported on October 1, 1975 that the Pound Sterling went down to its lowest level in its history, when Arab countries sold large quantities of the British pound in the world stock exchanges.

world inflation was not caused by the increases in oil prices; the inflation pressures were spreading throughout the world even before the oil crisis broke out. Some also pointed out that the cost of energy made up a relatively small proportion of the total gross national product (not more than 3%) and it should be easy to adjust to the new prices. These economists argue that even though almost three years have passed since the oil prices jumped up, not one of the consuming countries collapsed, and practically all of them have more or less adjusted to the new oil prices. Moreover, it would seem that most of the countries who were in the midst of a deep economic depression were recovering.

These specialists also seriously questioned the estimates of the surpluses of the producing countries, and the limited absorption level of these countries. One of the senior officials of the International Bank, Hollis B. Chenery, calculated that the price of a barrel of oil in 1980 would be about $8 (in 1974 prices), and that the producers' surpluses in that year would not be more than $300 billion. He added that the $300 billion would be only 5% of the total value of all stocks and bonds in the major OECD countries "or 2% of their fixed assets."

Another American expert emphasized that even should the United States have to pay about $28 billion annually for imported oil, the amount would be no more than 1.92% of the United States gross national product. The *Financial Times* of London declared that the impact of the high oil prices on the Western economies and on the Western money markets was much smaller than was thought at first. According to this paper the Western countries have successfully met the challenge of recycling the petro-dollars of the Middle East. What was necessary was the establishment of a mechanism for cooperation between the producers and the consumers.

Contrary to the estimates of the International Bank of 1974 that the OPEC countries' surpluses would amount to $170 billion by the end of the year, $650 billion by 1980 and $1,206 billion by 1985, the United States Treasury estimated that the surpluses in 1980 would amount to no more than $200 to $300 billion. Morgan Guaranty Trust Company of New York published conclusions of a research study which asserted that the nadir of the deficit in the balance of payments in the consumer countries caused by the high oil prices would be reached in 1975, and beginning with 1976 the deficit would commence to decline until 1979 when the producing and not the consuming countries would suffer from a deficit in their balance of payments.

It would seem that these great differences in the estimates of the surpluses did not stem from differences in methods and systems of research, but from other than pure economic and financial considerations. There could be no doubt that the first impact of the enormous increase in oil prices during the first three months of the crisis frightened all those who dealt with the balance of payments question and with the issue of surpluses, especially since the available data was very limited. It was, therefore, inevitable that the estimates would be somewhat exaggerated. But the basic facts have definitely not changed. The producing countries received and continue to receive enormous amounts of revenue. In spite of the grandiose multi-yearly development plans running into hundreds of billions of dollars, the huge purchases of products, whole technologies and services, they are not able to absorb even the major portion of their income. It is inevitable that the surpluses in their hands should constantly grow.

All the consuming countries are well aware that the only way to cure the economic sickness is to lower the oil prices. But in view of the position of the United States on the one hand and that of Western Europe and Japan on the other, two basic differences emerged, as mentioned above (Chapter 8). The United States wanted to consolidate all the consuming countries into a united front, in order to adopt measures which would induce the producers to reduce prices, after which ways and means would be found to stabilize the balance of payments and the utilization of the surpluses. Europe and Japan, on the other hand, were not ready to risk a struggle with the producing countries to reduce prices. They believed that through bilateral direct negotiations between themselves and the producers, and through other arrangements of investments and loans, they would succeed in solving the immediate current pressing problem. Only after normalization of relations would the price question be solved by the economic law of supply and demand. The consuming countries, therefore, dropped, at least for the time being, the question of prices and concentrated on the issues of surpluses and the recycling of the petro-dollars. The international financial institutions tried to extend, enlarge and augment their mechanisms which dealt with loans to countries which were in need of assistance.

We witnessed a race among the consumers, competing among themselves, to obtain the investments of the producing countries. The United States, which knew that she would be the first and most attractive candidate for the producers' investments, decided to adopt measures which would encourage the producing countries to invest in her economic undertakings. This apparently was the motivation for the new assessment of the surpluses which were publicized in Europe and in the United States, both as to the magnitude of the surpluses and the favorable conditions for their investments.

One of the devices which the consuming countries successfully exploited to bring back part of the surpluses was the sale of highly sophisticated military supplies and equipment in very huge quantities to the producers. Practically all the consuming countries with high productive military capacity were pursuing the producing countries—especially the big ones—and offered them arms, ammunitions of all sorts, including atomic plants, which ran into tens of billions of dollars. From an economic point of view, arms deals are the best and easiest and most desirable way to bring back the petro-dollars. (The fact that the saturation of the producing countries with heavy armaments was very likely to cause a conflagration among the nations of the Persian Gulf themselves, did not seem to disturb the arms peddlers). For armaments are economically non-productive; they do not increase the economic possibilities of the nations acquiring them, and within a relatively short time, become obsolete, and must be replaced by more modern ones. This would mean new sales by the consuming countries.

As was mentioned above, the IEA developed and adopted a many-itemed program aimed at defending the consumers from the producers. However, from a practical point of view the IEA remained ineffective. Yet one item in the program—a cut in consumption—yielded results. The reason for the cut was purely economic. In view of the high prices of oil, consumers reduced consumption drastically not as a part of the tactics of the struggle but out of practical savings. The outcome—especially in Europe—was very impressive indeed. All the estimates of the revenue and the surpluses of the producers were based on a 7%-8% annual increase in the consumption of oil. However, 1974 witnessed instead of an increase a general decrease. The cut in Europe reached 10% and in the United States and Japan about 3%. This decrease was one of the causes for the new assessments which appeared early in 1975.[3]

It would seem, however, that the new estimates of surpluses are also exaggerated downwards. A basic assumption in the new assessments was that the cut in consumption would continue in the same ratio up

(3) In October 1975 various sources reported additional reductions in consumption. An oil magazine in London reported that seven great oil importing countries (West Germany, France, Italy, Japan, Canada and the United States) imported during the first half of 1975 13% less than they imported in 1973, and the cause was primarily the high prices, a decrease of 2.6 million barrels a day. The general decrease during the two years since the oil embargo was imposed reached 22% in most of the West European countries. West Germany and France reduced consumption by 23%, Britain 24% and Italy by 17%. Japan reduced her imports by 12%. An oil monthly in New York reported that during the first half of 1975 production of crude oil in the Middle East was cut by 14%, from a daily production of 21.8 million barrels in 1974 to 18.8 million barrels in 1975. The same monthly reported that production in the OPEC countries fell during the same period by 16.7%. Nevertheless, OPEC increased prices by 10% at the end of September, 1975.

to the middle 'eighties. Consequently the revenue of the oil producing countries would be reduced while their ability to absorb their revenue would be increased, for funding economic development projects and for current budgetary needs. But these assessments ignored the fact that the ability of the consuming countries to cut consumption was not unlimited, unless they should decide on drastically curtailing their economic growth, increasing unemployment and lowering the standard of living. The ability to further reduce oil consumption would be dependent on developing and activating alternative sources of energy. Such development would involve not only the investment of prodigious sums of financial resources but also a readiness and determination for super efforts, including a confrontation with the producing countries. The consuming countries do not seem to be ready for either of the conditions. In fact consumption increased during the last part of 1976, and the predictions were that it would grow in 1977.

Practically all who deal with the questions of surpluses and re-cycling have somehow overlooked some basic aspects of the question. All the producing countries are vitally interested in ac-quiring from the developed consuming countries modern Western technology. They are determined to acquire this technology regard-less of price. They all openly admit that they need this technology for economic and other purposes. They demand guarantees (and they have succeeded in getting them) that in the process of acquiring this technology the consuming countries would supply not only the technological knowledge, but also the financial means for the further development of the oil industry and other industries and economic projects.

The outcome could be that the producing countries would become less dependent on the products of the consuming countries. They would be in full control of the production of petroleum and would compete with the consuming countries in all petroleum products and by-products. In such an eventuality, not only would the sur-pluses not be decreased, but most likely would be increased and in a rapid tempo.

To be sure, great wealth which makes possible planning and in-vestments, the import of new sophisticated equipment, purchase of foreign know-how and the employment of foreign experts is not the total answer to the needs of the producing countries. A basic requirement for efficient and effective utilization of equipment, knowledge and imported advice is a proper cultural, social and psychological background and tradition which would make possible the absorption and "digestion" of all the imported possessions.[4]

The conclusion must, therefore, be drawn that minimizing the magnitude of the surpluses problem by technical devices of recycling the petro-dollars through increased investments and loans is for all intents and purposes nothing but a delusion.

Because of the excellent position of the producers, and the badly divided condition of the consumers the former have exploited and exploit the situation for their own advantage. They increased prices through the well tried and established cartel tactics even when the supply of oil was much higher than the demand for it. In spite of all the various financial mechanisms and devices of the international financial experts, the producers gained full control over powerful economic forces, and they have acquired as a result great political influence. Thanks to the sophisticated schemes of the international experts, the consumers have slowed down considerably—if not to a complete stand-still—the development of alternative sources of energy. The producers at the same time have penetrated, through their investments, economic undertakings in the consuming countries, and increased their political influence by dictating to many great industrial concerns throughout the major countries their commercial policies, as illustrated by the Arab boycott against all companies and banks who were doing business with Israel even indirectly. While the consuming countries which supplied them with the huge surpluses became more and more helpless and dependent on them.

The international inflation which is the bane of the Western economies was not caused exclusively by the high prices of oil, but also by other products which are connected directly or indirectly with oil, by-products and derivatives. *Time* magazine reported that in 1974 the inflation in the United States reached 12%, and out of that 4% was caused directly by the high oil prices. As a result of the high oil prices, the inflation percentages were: in Japan 24, France and Belgium 16, Britain 18 and Italy 25.

(4) Saudi Arabia was apparently determined to exchange her billions of dollars, which she received for her oil, for American know-how. The Saudi Arabian Central Planning Organization was authorized by the Government on May 21, 1975 to adopt a five-year development program which would involve an expenditure of $144 billion. In order to attain their development goal the Saudi Arabians aimed at acquiring the most advanced technical and economic blue print. They attempted to import a half million technicians, managers, teachers and foreign workers. The planners hoped that by 1985 their country would become one of the most modern technological nations in the world. Early in March 1976, less than one year after the plan was announced, however, it was reported that Saudi Arabia had all but officially abandoned hopes of fulfilling the $144 billion five-year program. The country could not absorb the immense sums which had been allocated for the various items of the program. See footnote 1, Chapter 7.

10 Solutions

The Western world has been experiencing an energy crisis since October 1973, which in reality was a Middle East oil crisis. As a result of economic and other factors, the oil producing countries of OPEC gained the upper hand. They raised the posted prices of oil unilaterally, the last time at the end of 1976, and the consuming countries were helpless and incapable of doing anything about it. They raised the royalty rates, they increased their shares in the company profits, they raised their participation ownership in the companies from 25% to 60% and finally nationalized the foreign oil companies, and the latter were powerless and submitted. Without entering the discussion as to the exact role of the oil price in the world inflation, it is clear that the very rapid increases in the oil prices over a comparatively short period of time have contributed in considerable measure to the inflationary pressures, and prevented the consuming countries from overcoming the inflation. In spite of the various predictions in the United States and in Western Europe about the approaching end of the economic depression and the advance of the new prosperity, we are witnessing general economic hardships in most of the oil consuming countries; the economic recovery is not yet around the corner. Inflationary pressures are endangering many regimes in Europe and South America.

It is obvious that if the oil prices had gone down it would have been possible to slow down the galloping inflation, and even stabilize to some extent the general Western price structure. Instead we see substantial rises in unemployment, not only in the weak but also in the strong industrialized countries; but it is felt most heavily in the developing countries. Some of the Western European economic specialists have explained the reduction in oil consumption as the direct outcome of the economic depression which has engulfed the industrialized countries in spite of the considerable drop in the prices of some raw materials.

The consuming countries have tried, because of the assumption that the high oil prices were one of the most important—if not decisive—factors in the present economic crisis, and because of the fact that a stoppage of the flow of oil, or its limitation, would endanger their very existence, to find solutions for the energy problem through various instrumentalities which they devised in the last years. These were: the International Energy Agency, the Common Market, Arab League Dialogue and the International Conference for Economic Cooperation; but, so far, they yielded no tangible or other results. The reasons for their failure were stated in Chapter 8.

On the assumption that conditions are still serious and that it is imperative to find a solution to the energy problem—for otherwise the above mentioned efforts would not have been made and we would not have heard the frequent alarms from the most authoritative United States sources about the gravity of the situation—we shall attempt to examine some of the offered solutions. The aims of all of them are two: lower the price of oil and guarantee the secure, steady flow of the oil from the Middle East to the consuming countries.

A solution which was mentioned a number of times, all by American spokesmen, was a military invasion of the Middle Eastern oil fields—should the conditions resulting from either the high prices or from a cut-off of supplies cause "economic strangulation" (Kissinger's phrase)—in order to insure the flow of the oil at reasonable prices. The threats of military invasions which were first made by Secretary of State Kissinger and by President Gerald Ford were very general and did not specify the ways or the means for executing the possible invasion, nor the methods of activating—after the invasion—the oil industry. But commentators and scholars attempted to fill in the many and varied particulars and tried to persuade world public opinion that a military invasion was a practical possibility. It would seem clear that those who sent up the trial balloons of an invasion were aware of the insuperable problems and difficulties of executing such an undertaking and, therefore, never troubled to go into operational details.

It is perhaps possible, although it is not absolutely certain, that from a purely technical-theoretical point of view such an invasion could take place, but activating afterwards the very complex oil industry with its many branches and aspects—from production through marketing—in a hostile environment, places the whole plan in very serious doubt. Moreover, the very idea of a military invasion does not seem feasible in view of the relations between the United States and Western Europe. The sad and bitter experience of the United States with the air-lift in the October 1973 war would be an indicator of the magnitude of the problem. From a realistic point of view only the United States could think seriously—if merely in terms of resources and logistics—of an invasion possibility, and it would be inconceivable to assume that she would undertake such a project under the prevailing relations. In spite of all the gloomy predictions which American spokesmen made about the ever growing dependence of the United States on Middle East oil, the fact remains that in case of an emergency the United States could manage without Middle East oil. It would, therefore, not seem plausible that the United States would go out of its way thousands of miles to the Persian Gulf and invade the oil fields there in order to save Western Europe and Japan from economic strangulation, while these very countries refused to be saved. Such an invasion would cost hundred of billions of dollars which would make the oil to be produced more expensive than the possible alternatives. Moreover, it would be unthinkable that the Soviet Union, in spite of its great desire to continue with the detente policy and all that stems therefrom, would be standing on the side lines and allow the United States to do as she pleases in one of the most important global strategic regions, one in which the Soviet Union is struggling to gain a foothold and a degree of control.

Out of all these considerations we must come to the conclusion that a military confrontation between the consuming countries (in fact only the United States) and the producing countries was no more than a psychological tactic rather than a practical solution, and the threat of which, for all intents and purposes, was a complete fiasco.

A much simpler, although cruel, solution to the oil crisis would be for the consuming countries to surrender to the oil producers and comply with all their demands. The consumers would pay the high prices for the oil which would be determined by the producers. To do that the consumers would have to rearrange the portion of oil in their economies and its share in their national resources. Such a solution would inevitably cause widespread unemployment throughout the Western world and substantial lowering of the standard of living as well as economic growth.

In the previous chapter we dealt with the economic and financial difficulties which were caused by the huge surpluses which were amassed by the producers and with the difficulties of recycling the petro-dollars. Should the consuming countries accept the demands of the producers they would have to change, not only their economic status, but also their political position and adjust themselves to the new conditions which would follow from those changes. If the consuming countries would not react to the fateful challenge of the producers to their status, the producers would become the rulers of the new world order, and the industrialized nations would have to abide by the will of the producers.

It is possible that economically the consuming countries would adjust to the high oil prices and would encounter no particular hardship because of the general parallel increase in their own products and services; in other words the general inflationary pressures would cover all products. In such a situation it should be clear that the producers would try, and no doubt would succeed, in raising oil prices. In fact this was the major and basic demand of the producers at the conference of consumers and producers at the December 1975 meeting in Paris and at the December 1976 OPEC conference in Doha. They demanded that the oil and other raw material prices be based on an index of products and services which they must obtain from the industrialized (consumer) nations. The difficulties of the consumers would, therefore, remain, even if all prices should rise. Moreover, if one of the factors, if not the major one, in the world's economic hardships was the unbridled inflation, then the vicious circle of a price war between oil and products would create additional difficulties and would make economic recovery impossible. For the producers depend, at least equally, on the consumers for the supply of products and services, as much as the consumers depend on the producers for oil.

It seems that both the producers and consumers must come to some understanding and some workable arrangement in stabilizing prices based on a contest between the two strong economic blocs. Until now the consumers were split and hopelessly divided in groups of conflicting interests and objectives and, therefore, powerless to take measures which would bring some sense of balance in the situation. The producers, in spite of some basic differences among them, and in spite of the diverse objectives of the various groupings among them, have nevertheless been able to work as a unit and to stand as one solid entity against the consumers.[1] As a result OPEC obtained all its demands. It stands, therefore, to reason that the only way to solve the energy crisis is for all the consumers to unite into one consolidated unit with the clear aim of freeing themselves from absolute dependence on the producers on the one hand, and to adjust oil prices to the general economic development of both the producers and consumers on the other hand. From a strictly institutional framework and plan of action such an organization in fact exists, namely the International Energy Agency. Its program is composed of all the necessary elements: development and activation of alternatives to oil, reduction of oil consumption, basing reasonable prices for oil and guarantee prices for alternatives, sharing of all energy sources in times of emergency and assistance to developing countries in obtaining their energy needs.

If the consumers were as united and organized as the producers, with

(1) The Doha results may have jarred the OPEC unity; how serious the differences between the members were to OPEC's cartel power only time will tell.

determination to solve the energy problem, they would have at their command powerful economic means no less important and convincing than the oil resources of the producers. The three groups of the Western countries, United States, Japan and Western Europe, possess tremendous resources for a contest with the producers. They have the technology which the producers desperately desire, which they, and they alone could supply; they supply the various and multifarious products from heavy industry and sophisticated armaments to ordinary simple daily products which the producers use. They furnish the huge expanding markets for the producers' oil; and they are capable of absorbing the money surpluses in good and safe investments. The economic and financial structures of the producers and their economic development plans are based on their relations with the consuming countries. The latter, especially the United States, possess all the resources—technical, managerial and financial—to develop and activate alternatives to oil.

These great economic powers, available to the consumers, were not utilized until now because the consumers were not ready to use them; they somehow believed that they would not have to resort to them. They feared a confrontation with the producers. Experience, so far, shows that the producers succeeded in their efforts because they adopted measures and employed means which forced the consumers to comply, while the latter hesitated and were, therefore, at a complete loss.

That the producers fear a unity of the consumers and the resultant measures which they would adopt was evidenced by many declarations and threats made by different spokesmen of the producers each time a plan of action was proposed by the consumers.

After the producers have practically nationalized the oil industry in their territories, and the role of the concessionary companies was drastically reduced and limited, if not eliminated, it would have been logical that the governments of the consuming countries request the oil companies to cooperate with them in the contest with the producers. Instead of being producers and sellers of oil, the companies have become mere buyers, and they service the producing countries; they should, therefore, join the consumers and form a single front, which would be based on the full program of the IEA. This would bring stability of supplies, acceptable economic prices for energy resources and a permanent check on the inflationary pressures.

Up to the early 'seventies the balance of power between the consumers (more accurately the concessionary companies) and the producers was in the hands of the former; since then and particularly after October 1973 the balance has swung to the other side. It is, therefore, necessary to bring the relations between the two groups into balance which would serve equally both sides without a confrontation and without military threats. Such an objective would not be attained by surrender under threats of embargoes, nor by threats of military invasions. It would be attained by a readiness for an honest and legitimate contest tweeen the two sides. However, the present international political atmosphere is not conducive for such a contest. The Western world suffers from paralysis and lack of will to act. The Western countries seem to have lost their power of vision and the action necessary for realizing the vision. Because of the lack of determined energy and lack of planning on the one hand and a deep fear of the unknown future on the other hand, the Western countries are rapidly back-sliding—consciously or unconsciously—into fatal "adjustment" to existing conditions. The deep belief in international values and the readiness to fight for them have disappeared. Both physical and spiritual tiredness and general cynicism which is the product of despair and disappointment have paralyzed nerves and muscles alike.

Should the consuming countries reach a stage when they would be ready to find a solution for the energy problem which would be an inseparable part of the international and moral reevaluation, the solution would be the one here proposed.

Bibliography

In as short a study of the Middle East oil problems and issues as this one, it is obvious that it would be impossible to include a comprehensive bibliography. Readers are referred to the *Middle East, Oil and the Great Powers*, Third Edition, pp. 550-604, published by John Wiley and Sons, New York, 1974 for an over-all bibliography divided into the following categories: official documents (covering the various publications of the oil companies, of the producing countries, of the foreign governments involved, of the League of Nations and of the United Nations); books and articles by disinterested scholars and researchers and by representatives or agents of the companies and governments as well as by journalists; periodicals and newspapers; and bibliographies of bibliographies.

Some of the more recent books published since the above bibliography are hereby listed:

Adelman, M. A., *The World Petroleum Market*, Baltimore, 1973.

Anthony, John Duke (Ed.) *The Middle East Oil Politics and Development*, New York, 1975.

Fallon, Nicholas, *Middle East Oil Money and Its Future*, London, 1975.

Fesharaki, Fereidun, *Development of the Iranian Oil Industry—International and Domestic Aspects*, New York, 1976.

Ghanem, Shukri M., *The Pricing of the Libyan Crude Oil*, Malta, 1976.

Ion, D. C., *Availability of World Energy Resources*, London, 1976.

Klebanoff, Shoshana, *Middle East Oil and U. S. Foreign Policy with Special Reference to the U. S. Energy Crisis*, New York, 1974.

Mosely, *The Tumultuous World of Middle East Oil, 1890-1973*, London, 1973.

Russell, Jeremy, *Energy as a Factor in Soviet Foreign Policy*, Westmead, (England), 1976.

Rustow, Dankwart, and John F. Mimgo, *OPEC, Success and Prospects*, New York, 1976.

Rybczynski, T. M., (Ed), *The Economics of the Oil Crisis*, London, 1975.

Sampson, Anthony, *The Seven Sisters*, New York, 1974.

Tanzer, Michael, *The Energy Crisis: World Struggle for Power and Wealth*, New York, 1974 (?).

U. S. Federal Energy Commission, *The Relationship of Oil Companies and Foreign Governments*, Washington, 1975.

Vernon, Raymond, (Ed), *The Oil Crisis: In Perspective*, New York, 1975.